£1.30

IMPERIALISM IN THE ROMAN REPUBLIC

Edited by ERICH S. GRUEN
University of California, Berkeley

HOLT, RINEHART AND WINSTON
New York · Chicago · San Francisco · Atlanta
Dallas · Montreal · Toronto · London · Sydney

Cover illustration: Roman warrior. Iberian Peninsula, 200 B.C. *(Museo Arqueológico Nacional, Madrid; Foto Mas)*

Maps on pp. iv and v: Reprinted with permission of The Macmillan Company from *A History of Rome to* A.D. *565,* Fifth Edition, by Boak and Sinnigen. © Copyright by The Macmillan Company, 1965.

CONTENTS

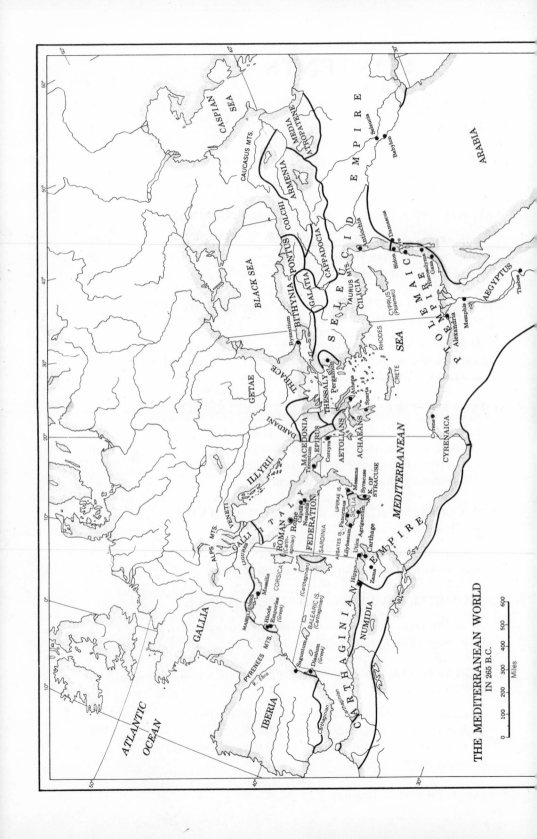

THE MEDITERRANEAN WORLD
IN 265 B.C.

Miles

0   100   200   300   400   500   600

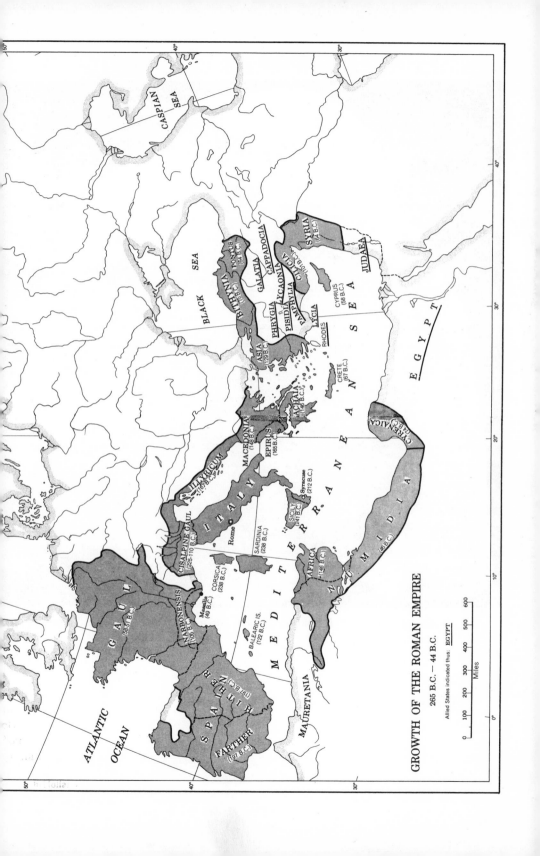

GROWTH OF THE ROMAN EMPIRE

265 B.C. — 44 B.C.

Allied States indicated thus: EGYPT

Miles

0   100   200   300   400   500   600

ATLANTIC OCEAN

CASPIAN SEA

BLACK SEA

MEDITERRANEAN SEA

EGYPT

GAUL
(58-51 B.C.)

NARBONENSIS
(105 B.C.)

Massilia
(49 B.C.)

SPAIN
HITHER
(206 B.C.)

FARTHER
(197 B.C.)

MAURETANIA

BALEARIC IS.
(122 B.C.)

CORSICA
(238 B.C.)

SARDINIA
(238 B.C.)

CISALPINE GAUL
(225-70 B.C.)

ILLYRICUM
(167? B.C.)

ITALY

Rome

SICILY
(241 B.C.)

Syracuse
(212 B.C.)

AFRICA
(146 B.C.)

NUMIDIA
(46 B.C.)

CYRENAICA
(96 B.C.)

MACEDONIA
(146 B.C.)

EPIRUS
(168 B.C.)

ACHAIA
(146 B.C.)

CRETE
(67 B.C.)

RHODES

ASIA
(129 B.C.)

BITHYNIA
(75 B.C.)

PONTUS
(64 B.C.)

GALATIA

CAPPADOCIA

PHRYGIA

LYCAONIA

PISIDIA

PAMPHYLIA

LYCIA

CILICIA
(102 B.C.)

SYRIA
(64 B.C.)

CYPRUS
(58 B.C.)

JUDAEA

Roman horseman. Iberian Peninsula, 206 B.C. *(Museo Arqueológico Nacional, Madrid; Foto Mas)*

INTRODUCTION

"It was not by accident or without knowing what they were doing that the Romans boldly struck out for universal dominion and rule—and accomplished their aim." The words were penned by the Greek historian Polybius writing at the conclusion of more than a century of Roman expansion and conquest. By 134 B.C. that lengthy but concentrated burst of activity had made Rome the unchallenged mistress of the Mediterranean. To Polybius, who observed a dominion that was secure and to all appearances complete, it was all logical and obvious. Fate had willed it; Rome had executed it.

Hindsight is the most seductive of historical faculties—and the most misleading. In 265, before Rome's first overseas venture, few Romans would have predicted or anticipated the conversion of the Mediterranean into a Roman lake. The "manifest destiny" might be acknowledged in retrospect; it was not postulated in advance. *Imperium* is a Latin word, but imperialism is a modern concept. The difference is significant and revealing. Rome created an empire, but she did not theorize about it. Wars needed to be justified, for the gods could not condone aggressive hostilities unless undertaken out of self-defense. But dominion following upon conquest was taken for granted. It received no elaborate explanations and elicited few misgivings. Cicero might criticize Asia for groaning under the burden of Roman taxes when Rome had brought peace and security to an area torn by endemic civil strife. But that too was hindsight. Similarly, when Virgil wrote that Rome's mission was "to spare the subjected and humble the haughty," he was looking upon an empire already fully formed. But Rome had launched her expansion without missionary zeal, without a self-conscious plan to civilize the world, without the comforting illusion of a "white man's burden." Nineteenth-century Britain may have been buoyed by a sense of superiority, a drive to bring superior culture to the "underdeveloped." Rome embarked on expansion with no such ambitions or illusions. The civilization of Carthage was at least as old as that of Rome. Greek civilization was much older. The Roman sense of superiority was the product of, not the motive for, war and conquest.

Rome's territory reached its broadest expanse in the second century A.D. when it extended from Britain to Arabia. The ultimate limits, however, are not our concern here; they were the issue of four centuries of expansion. The crucial period came at the beginning, between 264 and 134 B.C., when the Roman Republic burst its

Italian confines and subdued, in turn, Sicily, Sardinia, Africa, Macedon, Greece, and the Iberian peninsula. The process was slow and often halting. Trial and error rather than systematic plan marked the operations. Diplomacy was sometimes preferred to war; a friendly dependency might be more advantageous than a subject state. But by 134 cautious methods had been abandoned as unproductive and frustrating. Rome had adopted the policy of direct annexation. Troublesome states could best be managed by reducing them to the status of Roman provinces. Many additions of territory were to come; the spread of Roman culture was to reach much of the known world. Before the end of the Republic, Pompey the Great had subdued Asia Minor, Syria, and Judaea; Julius Caesar had pushed Roman frontiers to the Rhine by annexing the whole of Gaul; and Caesar Octavianus, the future emperor Augustus, had transformed the ancient kingdom of Egypt into his own private preserve. But the years 264 to 134 witnessed the emergence from Italian isolation, the first successes and failures in international diplomacy, and the development of the annexationist policy which determined all future expansion. At the outset of that era, most of the Mediterranean powers had barely heard of the city on the Tiber; at its conclusion, the once mighty Carthaginian empire, the savage tribes of Spain, and the proud Hellenistic monarchies all acknowledged the sway of Rome. How did it happen and why? The following pages will weigh certain explanations offered by some of Roman history's most distinguished students.

The problem is not made easier for us by the nature of the source materials. The works which are preserved and the sources on which they drew were all written from the vantage point of Rome. Imperialism observed from above would be a very different phenomenon if viewed from below. We do not possess the story as written by the Carthaginians or the Athenians or the Spaniards. It is no accident that we speak of the "Punic Wars" or the "Macedonian Wars." These were not names ascribed to the conflicts by the Carthaginians or the Macedonians. The Greek historian Polybius is the exception that proves the rule. He spent most of his adult years in Rome, a close friend and associate of Rome's leading statesmen and military conquerors. Indeed he was instrumental in implementing Rome's administrative settlement of Greece in 146. His view too was from above. It is the delicate and difficult task of modern historians to redress the balance and to examine Roman motivation outside the context of ancient apologists.

In 134 Romans could look upon their achievement with a sense of pride. No power had been able to withstand the force of Roman arms. But there was another side to the story. Scipio Aemilianus, it is reported, wept as he witnessed Carthage in flames, reflecting that a similar fate might be in store for Rome. Conquest had taken its toll on Roman character. A century later the historian Sallust could moralize on the subject: "When our state had grown powerful through toil and the practise of justice, when great kings had been subdued in war, when barbarian nations and mighty peoples had been subjugated by force, when all the seas and lands lay open, fortune began to grow cruel and cast confusion on all our affairs.

The lust for money and then for empire grew apace. At first the vices grew slowly and sometimes were punished; but later when the disease spread like a plague, the state was changed, and what had been a dominion of the highest virtue and equity was transformed into one of cruelty and intolerance." That power corrupts is a commonplace. The impact of imperialism on the domestic front is a matter to be dealt with in these pages.

"Empire" is probably a misnomer for Roman holdings in the Republic. It suggests order, structure, a consistent plan. The Romans, however, instituted no uniform system in the provinces. Relatively primitive Spanish tribes could not be treated in the same way as the sophisticated Greeks of the east. To some areas Rome transferred her own institutions; elsewhere previously existing structures were adopted. In the Republic, Rome was much more concerned with conquest and dominion than with organization. Governorships of foreign territories were temporary posts whose functions were performed by Roman magistrates or ex-magistrates. The Republic never escaped the notion that a provincial governorship was simply an appendage to an urban magistracy. Serious consideration of administrative problems had to await the advent of Augustus and the inception of an imperial bureaucracy. The reason lies largely in the origins of the empire. Overseas holdings were acquired piecemeal, each in its own context and circumstances. There was no master plan, no systematic pattern, no conscious program. "Empire" is an abstraction not readily susceptible to analysis. To Polybius the steps may have seemed logical and inescapable. But the Romans did not act as if the end were in view from the beginning. What motivated them to engage Carthage need not have applied to expansion into the Hellenic world. It has been the virtue of modern research to examine the stages in detail and in their own terms. The examination inevitably begets controversy, especially as regards the slippery questions of motivation and purpose. These are questions for the reader to ponder.

In 265 B.C. Rome was on the eve of overseas expansion. The Italian peninsula was now united under Roman hegemony. Through absorption, annexation, common citizenship, or treaty the Italian states were bound to Rome in common policy. Arnold J. Toynbee offers a lucid summary of the strengths and weaknesses of the Roman confederation at this juncture. The relative isolation of Italy from the areas conquered by Alexander gave Rome the time needed to extend her influence and consolidate her holdings at home. The city's central location in the peninsula, astride the Tiber, afforded a unique position for dominion and control. And Italy's central position in the Mediterranean basin enabled Rome to face both east and west. By 265 Roman legions, drawn from the peasantry and fighting for their city and homes, had already proved their skill under fire for generations. Rome won the loyalty of Italy, not only through force of arms, but through extension of the franchise and a sharing of institutions. But these advantages had corresponding disadvantages. The very centrality of Italy's situation and the absence of natural barriers, aggravated by the lack of a fleet, made the peninsula an inviting target for external threats. The institutions of a city-state and the mobilization of a citizen army were suitable for supremacy in Italy. But were the financial and economic resources of a city-state adequate for overseas expansion? Were its institutions adaptable to the role of an imperial power? The issues raised by Toynbee should be borne in mind throughout any study of Rome's era of expansion.

Once the toe of the Italian boot was under Roman suzerainty, Rome faced across the narrow Strait of Messina to Sicily. That island had for many generations been a bone of contention between Greeks and Carthaginians. In 264 Carthage appeared to have established a bridgehead at Messana just across the strait from Italy. Roman intervention, on appeal from Messana, sparked a war that was to last for more than twenty years. The decision to intervene was momentous and proved irreversible. For the first time Rome engaged forces beyond the shores of Italy. War with Carthage opened the path to conquest of the Mediterranean. Were the conflict and its consequences inevitable? Or may responsibility be assigned to one or the other of the parties?

H. H. Scullard stresses the tightness of the situation. A confrontation between two major powers is difficult to avoid when their spheres of influence are separated only by a narrow strait of water. When an incident occurred that afforded a pretext, Rome took advantage of it to cross the strait. But Scullard cautions against assumptions of Rome's aggressive intent. Carthage had already shown a policy of expanding commercial monopoly. Rome was concerned for her security, or at least for that of her allies in southern Italy. The action then was a precautionary measure designed to forestall Carthaginian ambition.

Some of Scullard's points may be granted. A Carthaginian garrison just off the shores of Italy must have caused uneasiness in Rome. But a theory that absolves Rome of blame and ascribes to her a defensive posture finds no favor with J. H. Thiel. He points to a treaty between Rome and Carthage which forbade Roman intervention in Sicily, a treaty which, he believes, was suppressed by Roman annalists. Hence Rome undertook her Sicilian adventure in full knowledge that she was violating treaty obligations. Moreover, Thiel argues, Rome's leaders cynically portrayed the appeal from Messana as a moral obligation to intervene in order to dragoon a reluctant populace into war. The imperial ambition can therefore be traced back to Rome's initial venture outside Italy.

M. Cary finds both of these approaches unsatisfactory. Aggressive ambitions on both sides suggest that a clash was inescapable. Cary points out, however, that previous relations between Rome and Carthage show little evidence of latent hostility. A comfortable, if not a warm, coexistence had been the rule. It required a peculiar series of events around Messana to draw the two powers into conflict. And even then reason and moderation could have effected a mutually acceptable arrangement. The war was by no means inevitable, and both sides share the guilt for permitting an unnecessary conflagration. In this view the inception of Roman imperialism began without forethought or conscious plan.

The second half of the third century B.C. witnessed two lengthy and grievous wars between Rome and Carthage. At their conclusion Rome had humbled Africa and annexed Sicily, Sardinia, Corsica, and Spain. In 201 Hannibal was defeated and Italy was safe but exhausted. Yet within a year Rome had embarked on a new venture, one that bid fair to be at least as exhausting and as dangerous: an invasion of the east and conflict with the great Hellenistic monarchies of Macedon and Syria. Rome would now have to contend with older, more prestigious, more established powers than herself. It is hardly surprising that to explain Rome's actions at this point has proved to be one of ancient history's most vexing problems. Scholarly controversy on the matter continues unabated. The issue is no minor one. Eastern expansion was eventually to bring the whole Greek world and the riches of Asia under the control of the Italian invader.

The classic statement on the subject was delivered by the greatest of Roman historians, Theodor Mommsen. Philip of Macedon had earlier cooperated with Hannibal against Rome. Now he had designs on Egypt, Greece, the Aegean, and Asia Minor. Rome had diplomatic dealings with many of these Greek states; she already harbored suspicions about Philip; and, most important, in Mommsen's eyes, she was unwilling to see the Greeks crushed under the heel of the Macedonian conqueror. The conflict with Philip was "one of the most righteous wars which the city ever waged." Roman philhellenism is suggested by the settlement that followed the war, a declaration of the freedom of the Greeks. The motives were admirable, but the policy mistaken. Greece was not readily capable of managing her own freedom. Rome's withdrawal after victory left a vacuum soon to be occupied by Antiochus of Syria, and Rome's forces had to engage in new conflict to protect the Greeks.

Maurice Holleaux agrees with Mommsen that aggressive ambitions played no role in inspiring a Roman *Drang nach Osten*. But he also rejects Mommsen's notion of philhellenism. Rome entertained no territorial desires, not because she loved the Greeks, but because she was largely indifferent to them. What stung Rome into action was concern for her own interests. News of a pact between Philip and Antiochus roused fears of a combined Hellenistic invasion of the west. The fear was groundless, but no less real for that. Rome felt the need to engage in what she regarded as preventive warfare. The protectorate of the Hellenes was really designed as a buffer to protect Rome.

Neither Mommsen's nor Holleaux's solution was found to be sufficient by E. Badian. Philhellenism, while it may have been felt by individuals, was never an arm of governmental policy. A union of Philip and Antiochus may have caused concern, but Rome could hardly have feared an invasion of Italy. The protectorate of the Greeks was a natural outgrowth of Rome's previous diplomatic attitudes. The Italians had for a long time looked to Rome for protection, a useful system for the suzerain whose obligations were loose and ill-defined. Rome could defend them when her own interests were at stake, or remain aloof when the situation was not urgent. A similar protectorate had been stretched over much of Illyria, across the Adriatic, in the latter third century. In this way Rome could extend her prestige without committing her vital interests. On this theory the clash with Philip was provoked when Roman hegemony over Illyria was challenged. In the course of conflict with Macedon and Syria Rome expanded the system logically to Greece, the Aegean, and Asia Minor. The "freedom of the Greeks" was neither philhellenism nor territorial ambition on the part of Rome. The Greeks could be expected to feel gratitude and act on behalf of their "liberator," but, on Rome's side, the reciprocal obligation need be discharged only when she felt her interests involved. It is Badian's suggestion, then, that Rome's entanglements in the east grew out of an adaptation of the Roman system as it existed in Italy.

Spain fell to Rome as a result of Carthage's defeat in 201 B.C. But the withdrawal of Carthage did not mean that Spain would now submit tamely to Roman overlordship. It was well over half a century before Rome was able to secure full control of the Iberian Peninsula. The military and political problems facing Rome were of a scale and nature completely different from those she encountered in the eastern world. Spaniards were organized, not in city-states or monarchies, but in half-civilized tribes, skilled in guerilla warfare and fiercely jealous of their autonomy. Rome's dealings with the Hellenistic world fitted her for ultimate hegemony over the lands of the Middle East. Conflicts in Spain proved to be the training ground for eventual Roman absorption of western Europe. In the course of those conflicts Rome compiled a record of brutality and treachery unparalleled in her history. The reasons are not easy to ferret out. Why should Rome's careful and, on the whole, respectable diplomatic dealings in the east have had no counterpart in her actions in the west?

It can be pointed out that the Spaniards were unlike Rome's previous opponents. They showed little concern for diplomatic niceties. Since treaties were signed as a consequence of defeat in war, a revival of strength justified scrapping contractual obligations and renewing hostilities. The faithlessness of the Spaniards dictated similar reactions from Rome. Such is the argument presented by Tenney Frank. Rome could deal with the Spaniards only by meeting them on their own terms; hence the cycle of cynicism, betrayal, and butchery. Her behavior reflected not so much a degeneracy of character as an adaptation to the particular circumstances called forth by the Spaniards.

A solution of this kind was repugnant to A. Schulten, who devoted almost a lifetime of study to Roman rule in Spain. Roman behavior is not to be excused by reference to the activities of the Spaniards. Rome's object from the beginning was economic and military exploitation. Revenues from the lucrative gold, silver, and copper mines proved an irresistible temptation. Roman governors were not content with exacting legitimate tribute, but adopted extortionate policies to fleece the provincials and line their own pockets. No less extortionate was the ruthless levying of troops to increase manpower for the conqueror. It hardly evokes surprise that Spaniards continued to resist tenaciously and caused frequent Roman losses until the subjugation of Numantia in 134 B.C. Schulten finds no reason but greed and frustration for the black record of Roman cruelty in the Iberian peninsula.

A different line of approach has recently been taken by A. E. Astin. Rome's ruthlessness is not mitigated by stressing the treachery of the Spaniards. On the other hand, notions of aggressive imperialism and conscious exploitation also fail to get to the heart of the matter. An attitude of mind, taken for granted, dictated the events. Rome did not understand the notion of peace without unconditional surrender. Negotiation and compromise were no solutions to a military situation. Hence treaties concluded on the battlefield by incompetent generals were continually rejected by the government at home. And Rome's generals were also her magistrates. The lack of a professional Roman officer class and the resiliency of the Spaniards caused continual warfare and a split between the senate and the generals. Thus, the basic structure of government and an underlying attitude toward war, in Astin's view, made the Spanish debacle inevitable.

For half a century after the defeat of Hannibal, the Carthaginians were quiescent. Rome had dismantled Carthage's military establishment, but had not annexed any of her territory. The chief beneficiary was Carthage's principal rival in Africa, the kingdom of Numidia. Massinissa, the Numidian monarch, had cooperated with Rome in the Hannibalic War and had profited from such collaboration. For the next generation and a half Massinissa periodically encroached on Carthaginian territory. Crisis after crisis produced appeals to Roman diplomacy, which generally resulted in settlements favorable to Numidia. The final confrontation came in the 140s. Carthage expressed a willingness to surrender. But Rome intervened by force and the results were definitive. Carthage was razed, its inhabitants enslaved, and resettlement within ten miles of the sea was forbidden. Africa was formally annexed as a Roman province. The decision was pregnant with consequences. A policy of maintaining a balance of power in Africa by playing off Carthage against Numidia, which had worked for half a century, was now abruptly abandoned. Client-states were not sufficient; Rome would now transform them into direct appendages and provinces. The action taken in Africa in 146 was repeated in the same year in the east: Greece and Macedon were put under the supervision of a Roman governor. Thus ended more than a century of trial and error in organizing foreign dependencies. The pattern set in 146 was in large part to determine the forms of all future Roman expansion. Motives for the conquest and annexation of Africa warrant careful scrutiny.

B. L. Hallward explains the Roman decision in terms of calculated policy. Rome had for a long time acquiesced silently or overtly in Numidian expansion at Carthage's expense. The fluid situation suited Rome's interests. As long as Numidia and Carthage were at loggerheads, both looked to Rome as an intermediary, and the balance of power in North Africa was maintained without the commitment of Roman arms. But the crisis beginning in the late 150s threatened to upset that balance. If Carthage were to capitulate to Massinissa, Rome would once more be faced with a major power in Africa, this time Numidia. Hence, on this view, Rome's destruction of Carthage and annexation of her territory had the object of keeping Carthage out of the grasping hands of Numidia. This theory has found wide acceptance.

It is possible, however, to arrive at a diametrically opposed solution. F. E. Adcock reviews a number of possibilities suggested by scholars, including that advocated by Hallward. He rejects the notion that Rome had any concern for the growing power of Numidia. Fear of Carthage was a more potent element in the decision. Whatever the realities of the Carthaginian threat, Cato's rantings that "Carthage must be destroyed" did not fall on deaf ears. Rome had already fought two deadly wars with that foe, and rumors of Carthage's revival, however ill-founded, provoked an inevitable Roman reaction. The role of irrationality in historical decision is not to be denied.

The destruction of Carthage in 146 and the simultaneous destruction of Corinth entailed the reduction of Africa and Greece to Roman provinces. The Mediterranean was directly and completely under Roman control. Carthage and Corinth had once been great commercial powers; their influence was now ended. Were Rome's motives for empire fundamentally economic?

Marxist historians have long ascribed economic motives to the Roman drive for imperial power. But one need not be a Marxist to acknowledge the economic benefits and changes accruing to Rome as a result of overseas expansion. The Russian anti-Bolshevik M. Rostovtzeff points to the fact that this expansion decisively altered the pattern of the Roman economy, which was formerly based on small peasant agriculture. The emergence of a commercial and financial class brought investments in "industry," trade, and profit-making landed estates. Pressure exerted by this class could have an impact on state policy, particularly in regard to Roman ventures in the Mediterranean and the elimination of commercial rivals.

This analysis has not persuaded all scholars. Among the doubters is E. Badian, who regards economic considerations as a modern obsession wrongly foisted upon the ancient world. The Romans thought in terms of strategy and politics, not profits. The spoils of war were the products of victory, and were taken for granted as the conqueror's right; but they did not supply the motive. Badian examines the key passages in the ancient sources that are customarily taken to prove economic motivation and shows that they can be subjected to a very different interpretation.

Finally, it is of value to step back and survey the course of Roman imperialism as a whole. What were its presuppositions? What was its character? What were its effects on Rome and Italy? In the initial selection in this book, Toynbee raises the question of whether the institutions of a city-state are capable of adaptation to the role of an imperial power. R. E. Smith, in glancing at the course of Roman expansion in this period, answers in the negative. Rome was unable to escape a mentality built up in her early wars for self-preservation in Latium and Italy. The goal was simply to weaken her neighbors, render them harmless, and bind them to her in common policy. This attitude was then carried abroad as well. It explains why Rome was content to humble real or potential enemies and reluctant to annex territory. The policy was one of self-defense and a minimizing of obligations, reflecting a city-state mentality. For this reason, Smith argues, Rome had to be summoned again and again to a reluctant undertaking of war. Lack of a feeling of responsibility for foreign dependencies marked Roman policy; Rome preferred to keep them at a distance rather than organize or administer them. Consequently, during the Republic the city-state never attained the attitude of a genuine world power.

E. Badian takes the analysis further and deeper. He distinguishes Roman policy in the east from that in the west. Rome eschewed annexation and preferred diplomacy in the east, because of the nature of Hellenistic society and the power of Greek public opinion. In the tribal areas of the west, where conditions were different, Rome showed no such scruples. Like Smith, Badian recognizes that the city-state was not prepared to assume the responsibilities of imperial organization. But this did not mean that Rome was concerned only with self-defense and with keeping foreign powers at arm's length. Aristocratic pride and desire for acknowledged hegemony underlay Roman policy in both east and west. While avoiding actual annexation and administrative responsibility wherever possible, Rome made sure to extend her visible influence and insisted upon the fulfillment of obligations due her from states under her protectorate. The domestic political system based upon respect and duties owed by clients to their aristocratic patrons was transferred automatically to the sphere of foreign policy.

Sallust wrote that imperialism wrought harsh and unwelcome changes in Roman character and society. In the concluding selection A. H. McDonald surveys the monumental effects which expansion abroad had upon internal conditions in Italy. The opening of foreign horizons wrenched Rome out of her traditional peasant economy. An industrial and commercial class was fostered through new overseas connections. The city of Rome became bloated with an indigent urban population moving in from the countryside. Large landed estates designed for capitalistic profit replaced the small grain-growing farms. A new cosmopolitanism, a quicker pace of life, and a flourishing culture spurred by Greek models became features of Roman society. But there were darker sides in the picture. Vine and oil plantations forced out the yeoman farmers; growing numbers of unemployed proletarians crowded the city; slaves from abroad replaced Italian free men on the land. This had serious repercussions in the military situation. A citizen army drawn from property owners became increasingly inadequate for policing overseas holdings and for waging lengthy, incessant, and distant wars. Deadly and unprofitable campaigns, particularly in Spain, began to rouse resentment among conscripted soldiers. The leadership discredited itself in the Iberian peninsula, not merely by its behavior toward the Spaniards but, more significantly, by military failures, to which Rome had not been accustomed. The result was social unrest and revolution. Roman imperialism, like all imperialisms, was a mixed blessing.

In the reprinted selections footnotes appearing in the original sources have in general been omitted unless they contribute to the argument or better understanding of the selection.

The name ARNOLD J. TOYNBEE (b. 1889) is celebrated well beyond the confines of classical scholarship. Toynbee's massive *Study of History,* a work of creative insight and originality, has had a powerful impact on a wide audience. The criticisms of some professional historians have not diminished the scope and grandeur of his conception. Toynbee is at home with a multitude of civilizations, both ancient and modern. But his training and his surest touch is in the world of classical antiquity. His recent two-volume work, *Hannibal's Legacy,* is the product of a half century of research and thought. In this selection he reviews the situation and attitudes of Rome just prior to her initial expansion outside the Italian peninsula.*

Arnold J. Toynbee

Rome on the Brink of Expansion

In uniting Peninsular Italy politically round herself, Rome had achieved something that no other state, based either in Italy or outside it, had ever achieved in Italy before. The enterprise was a difficult one intrinsically. For, in the age before the Roman conquest and the subsequent diffusion of Latin, the Italian peninsula was a mosaic of peoples speaking a number of different languages. By contrast, European Greece had been linguistically homogeneous since before the rise of the Hellenic Civilisation. On the mainland, at any rate, dialects of Greek had superseded all previous local languages in the course of the second millennium B.C. Linguistic unity has often provided a foundation for political unity. Yet European Greece remained

politically disunited until its incorporation in the Roman Empire. This contrast between the linguistic and political histories of the two peninsulas makes Rome's achievement in Italy all the more impressive.

The last stage in the completion of Rome's enterprise had been bound up with the defeat of the most serious of all the attempts that had been made to unite Italy from outside. Pyrrhus had commanded the resources of a united and enlarged Epirus. Competing war-lords in Continental European Greece, Ptolemy the Thunderbolt and Antigonus Gonatas, had given him additional ships and men as a cheap price for at least temporarily getting rid of him. Even the distant and hard-pressed Antiochus I had given him money.

*From *Hannibal's Legacy* by Arnold J. Toynbee, published by Oxford University Press, 1965, vol. I, pp. 267–274, 281, 289–294, 301–302. Footnotes omitted.

He had been invited into Italy by Tarentum, the second largest city-state in the Peninsula, surpassed, so far, only by Rome; and, besides Tarentum and her satellite Italiot Greek city-states, Pyrrhus had had, as allies, Tarentum's non-Greek South Italian neighbours—Calabrians, Lucanians, Bruttians, and Samnites—who had made common cause with Tarentum and Pyrrhus against the threat presented by Rome to all Italian states that she had not yet subjugated. Yet this unprecedentedly comprehensive and powerful coalition had not been consolidated into a counter-commonwealth, though a permanent union was the one thing that would have given the still independent South Italian states a chance of survival. About two hundred years earlier, the Etruscans' more desultory and casual attempt to unite Italy from inside had likewise come to nothing. As for the Syracusans, they had never got farther than an intermittent conquest of their fellow Greek colonists in the toe of Italy and a temporary acquisition of the naval command over the Adriatic Sea. Against the foil of these failures, Rome's achievement stands out. If we look for its causes, we shall find at least some of them in a coincidence of geographical good fortune with statesmanship.

One reason why Rome's enterprise escaped being nipped in the bud, as the Chalcidians' enterprise was nipped by Sparta, is to be found in the geographical accident that Rome and her earliest field of expansion in the Central Italian lowlands lay just beyond the range at which a power based on the heart of the Hellenic World, in Continental European Greece or the Aegean, could have brought its full strength to bear against Rome under the logistical conditions of the Pre-Industrial Age. This geographical good fortune might not, however, have availed if a piece of political good fortune had not come to its

aid. By 334 B.C.—the date at which the Macedonian Alexander crossed the Hellespont—Rome's commonwealth-building enterprise had gone about as far in the Central Italian lowlands as the Chalcidians' comparable enterprise had gone on the north coast of the Aegean when Sparta intervened there in 382 B.C. Let us suppose that, instead of turning eastwards, Alexander had turned westwards, crossed the Straits of Otranto instead of the Dardanelles, and joined forces with his namesake, uncle, and half-brother-in-law, Alexander of Epirus, whose landing in Italy was almost simultaneous with Alexander of Macedon's invasion of Asia. Even Livy, who has contended that Rome would have been more than a match for the Macedonian Alexander, would hardly have maintained that she would not have succumbed to a joint attack by the two Alexanders, with nearly the whole military power of Continental European Greece at their command. No doubt the Macedonian Alexander would have met, in Italy, with stiffer resistance than, in his actual eastward trek, he encountered anywhere to the west of the Caspian Gates. Yet it is hard to believe that the inchoate Roman Commonwealth would not have been broken, considering how near it came to being broken by Pyrrhus more than half a century later. Pyrrhus's resources were not comparable to Alexander the Great's, and, by the time of his landing in Italy (280 B.C.), Rome had used the previous thirty-three years to wear down the power of Samnium and thereby build herself up into being the predominant power in the Italian Peninsula. If in 334 B.C. the two Alexanders had achieved what Pyrrhus just failed to achieve in 280–275 B.C., all Italy might ultimately have become Greek-speaking, as all Anatolia ultimately did in consequence of Alexander's historical Asian conquests; and then the Greek language, instead of the Latin, would have spread to the Atlantic coasts of the Old World.

Rome was doubly favoured by Fortune in the distance that separated her from Pella and in the orientation of Alexander's ambitions. Yet Fortune cannot claim more than part of the credit. Her gift to Rome was the negative one of leaving her free to pursue her enterprise unimpeded by hostile intervention from outside Italy until Pyrrhus intervened at the eleventh hour, when it was already too late. The same gift of geographical remoteness had been granted to the Etruscans as well; but that had not been enough to enable the Etruscans to anticipate Rome in imposing political unity on Italy.

Rome had a second piece of geographical good fortune in finding herself situated on the borderline between the Mediterranean maritime world of city-states and this world's hinterland of relatively backward village-communities. The hills on which Rome is built stand in the North-West Italian lowlands. To the south-west the shore of the Tyrrhene Sea is almost in sight; to the north-east the foothills of the Sabine highlands are in full view. The highlanders, being backward culturally as well as politically, were not only conquerable by an organised civic community, such as Rome was; they were also malleable and assimilable, since they were peoples without long memories of past glories—in fact, "peoples without histories." For them—in contrast to the city-state communities in Etruria, Latium, and Campania, not to speak of Magna Graecia—the forfeiture of their separate political identity was not a very painful loss, whereas their incorporation in the body politic of a successful city-state, such as Rome was, gave them the entry into the great world of Mediterranean civilisation. . . . Rome took full advantage of this

situation. She first attracted sympathy and support among the lowlanders by presenting herself as the champion of the city-state way of life against culturally backward highland peoples, and she then enlarged her own body politic by incorporating in it, *en masse,* a number of highland peoples: Sabines, South-Western Vestini, Praetuttii, Picentes. . . .

Thus Rome occupied a central geographical position both in the Tyrrhene lowlands of Peninsular Italy and in the Peninsula as a whole. Rome's position was also a central one in the Mediterranean basin. In respect of this wider field, only Rhegium, Messana, and Syracuse were more centrally situated than Rome was, but none of those three cities combined, as Rome did, the advantage of centrality with the complementary advantage of easy access to a continental hinterland. If Alexander had conquered Italy, he would, we may be sure, have planted on the site of Rome a new Greek city, named after himself, to serve as the capital of his dominion in the Peninsula, as the historical Alexandria-on-Nile did serve Alexander's Ptolemaic successors as the capital of their dominion in Egypt. If that had happened, Alexandria-on-Tiber would be one of the World's famous cities today, and its original name 'Rome' would have fallen into the oblivion that has overtaken Alexandria-on-Nile's original name "Rhacôtis."

Rome's situation in relation to the River Tiber and its basin and hinterland was the only one of her pieces of geographical good fortune that was peculiar to Rome herself. She was also fortunate in being situated in the Italian Peninsula's relatively productive north-western lowlands; but on this score there were other Italian communities that were more fortunate than Rome was. The territories of the city-states of South-Eastern Etruria lay in the same belt of volcanic soil as the original nucleus of the

Ager Romanus, while North-Western Etruria contained the broad plough-lands round Siena and the iron-ore in the mainland territory of Populonia and on the adjacent island of Elba. But no land in either Etruria or Latium was so productive as the volcanic and alluvial soils of the Campanian plain, which was indeed the best agricultural land in all Peninsular Italy except, perhaps, the smaller patch of alluvium in the lower basin of the River Crathis, on the under-side of Italy's 'instep.''

This brief survey of Rome's geographical advantages leads to the conclusion that, after we have given these their full weight, we must look beyond them to human factors if we are to understand the causes of Rome's political success. The main credit for this is attributable to Roman statesmanship; and this was successful because it was inspired, in an unusually large measure, by the two virtues of generosity and persistence.

Rome showed her generosity in both the financial and the constitutional terms on which she incorporated in her Commonwealth the conquered peoples of Peninsular Italy during the seventy-five years, ending in 266 B.C., that it took her to expand her dominion from the lower Tiber basin over the rest of the Peninsula. She did not reduce any of her conquered adversaries to serfdom, as Sparta reduced some of hers. She did mulct some of them of land, partly for the plantation of additional Roman tribes and new Roman and Latin colonies, and partly for the laying out of new through-roads. But, for the most part, her terms for communities that she bound to herself by permanent alliances were that they should resign to Rome the conduct of their foreign relations and should contribute military or naval contingents or both, on fixed quotas, to Rome's armed forces, when Rome went to war.

Like Sparta, and unlike Athens, Rhodes, and possibly Carthage too, Rome forbore from exacting tribute from her satellite communities. Rome also followed a different policy from any of these other four empire-building Mediterranean city-states in the large-scale extensions of her own citizen-body that she made by partially incorporating subjugated communities in it.

This reception of some or all of the munia of Roman citizenship was sometimes imposed on conquered peoples against their will and was regarded by both parties, at the time, as being a precaution taken by Rome in order to secure her hold over the partially incorporated community rather than as being the sharing of a privilege. Roman citizenship, even of the lowest category, did carry with it certain personal rights; but these rights did not come to seem particularly valuable until a later stage, when Rome had become mistress of the whole Mediterranean World and when the possession of Roman citizenship had come to be the only effective protection against the arbitrary and tyrannical behaviour of Roman magistrates in that age. In the age before the Romano-Carthaginian Double War of 264–201 B.C. it did not seem like a privilege to be made subject to the duties and burdens entailed in Roman citizenship without being given simultaneously the rights of voting in the Roman national assemblies and of standing for the Roman public offices. Yet, as has been pointed out already, the imposition of Roman citizenship, even on the least favourable terms, was not by any means an unmitigated loss for a backward people such as the highland Sabines were. It also gave them something of positive value: an induction into civilisation.

Moreover, the partial incorporation of non-Roman communities in the Roman citizen-body did not take place on unfavourable terms in all cases. If the incorporated community was a city-state, it was allowed as a rule to retain its local civic self-government as a non-sovereign municipality within the political framework of the sovereign Roman state; and the dual citizenship enjoyed by peoples that became Roman municipes on these terms was not always confined, on the Roman side of it, to "citizenship without the vote." There were cases . . . in which a community incorporated in the Roman citizen-body was not only allowed to retain its own local civic self-government, as Capua, for instance, was allowed in 338 (335 or 334) B.C., but was also given, as Aricia, for instance, perhaps was in the same year, the active Roman franchise as well as the passive rights and duties that citizenship without the vote carried with it. In the third place, the partial incorporation of communities in the Roman citizen-body did not always take place compulsorily. There was at least one case in which foreign communities towards which Rome felt well disposed were given the choice between retaining their full separate communal identities as sovereign allies of Rome's and being partially incorporated in the Roman citizen-body. This was the choice that was offered to three Hernican city-states—Aletrium, Verulae, and Ferentinum—that had remained loyal to Rome when the rest of the Hernici had broken the terms of their alliance with Rome by going to war with her in 307 (307/6 or 306) B.C. It is significant, however, that, in this case, all three communities that were offered a choice chose to retain their existing status of being Rome's sovereign allies.

Rome's second political virtue, her persistence, shone out, in the last phase of her unification of Peninsular Italy, by contrast with Pyrrhus's volatility. Pyrrhus never disciplined himself to carry one enterprise through to a successful conclusion before allowing his energies to be diverted to another. He switched over from an Italian enterprise to a Sicilian one, from the Sicilian one back to the Italian one, from this to a Macedonian one, and from that, again, to a Peloponesian one, before he had achieved decisive results in any of these successive fields; and the consequence was that, when he met his death in the streets of Argos, he left no permanent achievement behind him. In contrast to the volatility of a Pyrrhus and a Demetrius the Besieger, the Roman oligarchy practised the persistence of a Philip II, a Ptolemy I, and an Antigonus Gonatas—with the immense additional advantage that the continuity of its policy did not depend on the duration of a precarious individual life or on the uncontested transmission of a crown to a successor. Like Philip II and Ptolemy I, the contemporary Roman oligarchy advanced one step at a time, taking care, each time, to secure the ground gained in the last step before taking a new one.

One of the not least noble and admirable features of the domestic history of Rome is its way of taking, for the most part, a quiet and steady course. It eschews feckless changes and violent revolutions. Its development is constant, purposeful and organic.

This is true, not only of Rome's domestic history, but also of the conduct of her foreign relations. . . .

Like all human institutions, the Roman Commonwealth had its weak points, well-built though it was. These weaknesses were brought to light by the test of the Double War of 264–201 B.C. and its sequel. They were of three kinds: geographical, economic, and politico-administrative.

The Roman Commonwealth's chief geographical weakness in 266 B.C. was Peninsular Italy's lack of natural frontiers.

The appearances to the contrary on the map are delusive. In reality Italy is no exception to the general rule in the Oikoumenê west of the western border of India. From there to the Atlantic there is, as has been observed, no country except Egypt that can be insulated strategically and therefore also politically. . . .

In 266 B.C. Rome found herself in a situation like the First Persian Empire's after Cyrus's annexation of Western Anatolia up to its frontage on the Aegean and on the Black Sea Straits, or like Macedon's situation after Philip II had brought the whole of Continental Greece except Lacedaemon into his Confederation of Corinth. Both the Persian Empire and Macedon had then soon discovered, by experience, that a coastline is not an automatic political insulator. The Achaemenidae had learnt that their hold on Western Anatolia was not secure so long as the islands in the Aegean, and the mainland of European Greece beyond them, remained politically independent. Inversely Philip had learnt before his death—and had bequeathed the lesson to Alexander—that the control which he had established over all but one of the states in Continental Greece would still be precarious so long as the Persian Empire continued to possess naval bases along the Mediterranean coasts of Asia and Egypt from which dissident movements in Greece could receive support. Rome's incorporation of the south-eastern extremity of the Italian Peninsula in her Commonwealth exposed her to the risk of being involved in corresponding complications. From Rhegium it was only a stone's throw to Sicily, and from Lilybaeum it was only a short sea-passage to Carthage. In the other direction the Straits of Otranto were also not broad enough to insulate Tarentum and Brundisium from Corcyra, and Corcyra was an off-shore island hugging

the coast of Continental European Greece. The Italiot and Siceliot Greek communities had, many times over, sought and received aid from their Continental European Greek kinsmen against the Carthaginians and the Oscans, before Rome had loomed up over their north-western horizon. Pyrrhus's intervention had been merely the last and the most formidable in the series. When a power from beyond the borders of Peninsular Italy had disputed the completion of the Roman conquest of the Peninsula, other foreign powers might dispute the maintenance of Roman rule there. Within two years of the incorporation of the residue of Peninsular Italy in the Roman Commonwealth, this possibility was brought home to Roman minds by the Mamertines' appeal for Roman help against their Carthaginian and Syracusan adversaries who were closing in on Messana. . . .

In Italy, agriculture was still being carried on in its traditional form, as subsistence farming; and this old-fashioned economic system was the basis of the state's military strength, since its military manpower was provided by its peasantry. But this Romano-Macedonian economy was an anachronism in the Hellenic World of the day. By this date, parts of the Hellenic World had already gone through two successive economic revolutions. In Ionia, the states round the Isthmus of Corinth, Magna Graecia, and Attica, subsistence farming had given way to cash-crop farming, commerce, and industry as far back as the seventh and sixth centuries B.C.; and, in the colonial area that had been opened up in the Western Mediterranean by Levantine enterprise, cash-crop farming had been raised to a higher power by being taken out of the hands of a free peasantry and organised in plantations worked by slave-labour. The earliest instance, known to us, of this inhuman high-powered method of cash-crop farming is its introduction in the territory of the Siceliot Greek colonial city-state Akragas in 480 B.C. It was adopted by the Carthaginians and was practised by them on a larger scale in the North-West African territory that they brought under their rule from about 450 B.C. onwards.

Meanwhile, Rome had not transformed her antique peasant economy to keep pace with these economic innovations at her doors. She had merely extended its range by military conquests. She had won new land for her own peasantry at the expense of her defeated opponents and at the same time she had attached to herself, by diplomacy or by force, a host of Italian communities that were still in the same stage of economic development as Rome herself. Probably this old-fashioned economy, which was still the standard type in Peninsular Italy, would not have long survived Rome's political unification of the Peninsula and her increasing participation in the life of the rest of the Hellenic World, even if there had been no Romano-Carthaginian Double War. As things turned out, the military demands on the Roman and ally peasantry that were made by this war, and especially by its second bout, wrecked the subsistence-farming economy of Peninsular Italy in the course of the next two generations after the completion of the political unification of the Peninsula in the Roman Commonwealth; and this was a practical demonstration that the Commonwealth's economic foundations had been too weak to bear the weight of its political superstructure in a geographical situation that made it impossible for a politically united Italy to keep out of the arena of Hellenic international power-politics. . . .

The Roman Commonwealth's chief administrative weakness was that, in the administrative organisation of a country as large and populous as Peninsular Italy was in 266 B.C., the Roman Government continued to rely upon a traditional institution the city-state, which had originally come into existence as an instrument for administering far smaller territories and populations.

Before the invention of present-day mechanical means of communication—telegraphs, telephones, radio, railways, automobiles, aircraft, and the rest—the problem of administering a country on the scale of Peninsular Italy as a single unit was a formidable one. The Romans did make one magnificent technical contribution towards solving this problem. They followed up the progressive extension of their conquests and alliances by progressively extending a network of trunk-roads radiating from the City of Rome in all directions. In 266 B.C. this network was still under construction. Since 312–311 (311/10–310/9 or 310–309) B.C. Rome had been linked with Capua, the second greatest city in the Ager Romanus and in the Commonwealth as a whole, by a pair of roads, the Via Appia and the Via Latina, which diverged just after their exit from Rome but converged again on the near side of the bridge over the River Volturnus at Casilinum. It is unlikely that the Via Appia had already been prolonged from Capua to Tarentum and thence to Brindisi, the port of embarcation for Greece and the Levant, which was this road's eventual terminus; and it is certain that Rome was not yet linked with Ariminum, the Commonwealth's northeast frontier-fortress on the Adriatic coast, since we know that the construction of the Via Flaminia was not begun till 220 B.C. All the same, enough progress in Roman road-building had been achieved by the year 266 B.C. to make it certain that the Roman Government could and would complete the network eventually. The construction of a network of trunk-roads on this scale was something quite beyond the traditional purview of a city-state government, and the Roman Government has justly been given great credit for having made this far-sighted new departure to meet its expanding Commonwealth's new administrative needs. Unfortunately, this was the only radical innovation that it did make in a situation that demanded many others besides. . . .

[The] Roman feat of constructing a Peninsular Commonwealth out of nothing but city-state materials was a remarkable one. It was, however, a *tour de force;* "it required the adaptation of institutions through the diversion of them from their original purpose to quite different purposes"; the results were sometimes different from what had been intended; and the structure was therefore subject to continual stresses and strains. These might prove dangerous if its fabric were ever to be put to a severe test—and Roman statesmanship could not count on being able to steer clear of this danger, considering that the Italian Peninsula was, geographically, an integral part of the Mediterranean World, and that its coasts, so far from being "natural frontiers," were highly "conductive" in the electrician's meaning of the word.

The first and crucial step in Rome's expansion outside Italy came in the initial war with Carthage. Whether or not this step was conscious and bespoke imperial ambition is a question still much debated. H. H. SCULLARD (b. 1903), professor of ancient history at King's College, London, and author of many works on Roman Republican history, addresses himself to this problem. In Scullard's view, Rome's action was inspired not by motives of territorial conquest, but by the need to protect Italy from an imminent Carthaginian threat. His major books include *Roman Politics, 220–150 B.C.* and *The Etruscan Cities and Rome.**

H. H. Scullard

Defensive Imperialism

Carthage had . . . won an overseas Empire which she selfishly exploited. The old Phoenician colonies abroad assumed much the same relation to her as the Libyphoenician towns in Africa. In Sardinia and southern Spain some of the natives were reduced to subjection; the rest were exploited commercially and supplied mercenary troops. In Sicily the Carthaginians had to tread still more warily, to avoid driving the whole island into the arms of her enemy Syracuse. The Punic province in the west gradually embraced some native and Greek cities, but these retained their internal autonomy and paid a tithe on their produce instead of supplying troops. Further, Carthage had to keep an open market in her Sicilian province. On the whole the condition of her subjects, though tolerable, was far inferior to that of most of the allies of Rome, who had infused her federation with a feeling of loyalty and imposed no tribute. The subjects of Carthage had no real bond, although common interests might sustain their loyalty for a time. Like the members of the Naval Confederacies of Athens they became increasingly dependent on their mistress without sharing in the advantage which the Greeks had enjoyed of all entering into relation with their leader at approximately the same time.

During this period of external expansion Carthage first came into contact with Rome. The intermediaries were her Etruscan allies, whose ports in Italy had long

*From H. H. Scullard, *A History of the Roman World, 753 to 146 B.C.* (London: Methuen & Company, Ltd., 1951), pp. 136–137, 141–145. Footnotes omitted.

been open to Phoenician merchants. The product of such trade is seen in the rich seventh-century tombs at Caere and Praeneste: silver and gilded bowls, painted ostrich eggs, and ivory plaques like those made for Solomon's temple by Tyrian artists. When the Etruscan dynasty was driven from Rome, Carthage struck a treaty with the new Republic. A copy of this treaty, engraved on brass, was preserved in the Treasury at Rome and was known to the historian Polybius. It was obviously the work of Carthage, as all the restrictions imposed were in her favour; only Rome's lack of commercial interests can explain why she accepted it. The Romans agreed not to sail south, and perhaps west, of the Gulf of Tunis, unless driven by stress of weather or fear of enemies; men trading in Libya or Sardinia were to strike no bargain save in the presence of a herald or town clerk; any Romans coming to the Carthaginian province in Sicily should enjoy all rights enjoyed by others. Thus Carthage was already enforcing the policy of a *mare clausum*: Numidia, Morocco, and the Straits of Gibraltar were perhaps closed: conditions of trade in Libya and Sardinia were restricted, though Carthage was not yet strong enough to claim a monopoly there or to close western Sicily. Further, it is assumed that the ports over which Rome had any control were to remain open. In return for these substantial advantages Carthage merely pledged herself to abstain from injuring certain towns in Latium. When this treaty was renewed, probably in 348, Rome allowed Carthage to stiffen up the conditions very considerably. By the new agreement Roman traders were excluded from Sardinia and Libya and from the western Mediterranean from the Gulf of Tunis to Mastia (Cartagena) in Spain; Carthaginian Sicily and Carthage itself alone remained open. Thus the new Republic willingly sacrificed any commercial

interests which Rome may have had under the Etruscan régime; for many a long year her thoughts turned landwards while her future rival was transforming the western Mediterranean into a Carthaginian lake. . . .

The early treaties between Rome and Carthage were treaties of friendship and for trade, formed to limit their spheres of influence. But in 306 the two Republics had entered into a closer political agreement which debarred the Carthaginians from interfering in Italy, and the Romans in Sicily. Carthage again negotiated with Rome in 279; no defensive alliance was struck, but an emergency measure was designed, chiefly to keep Pyrrhus in Italy. During the war Carthage neither received nor asked for help, not wishing to bring Romans into Sicily; Rome also kept to herself.

In 272 a puzzling incident occurred. When the Romans were besieging Tarentum, which was still held by Pyrrhus' lieutenant Milo, a Carthaginian fleet suddenly appeared in the harbour, but quickly sailed off again. Had it come in reply to an appeal from Milo or on its own initiative; to help the Romans or to capture Tarentum? Later Roman writers accused Carthage of having tried to seize Tarentum, alleging that the action was a breach of treaty rights; but the Carthaginians had not tried to land. Indeed, so far from acting contrary to the agreements, the Punic admiral may have sailed up in accordance with Mago's treaty to see whether he could help the Romans. It is perhaps most likely that the Carthaginians were reconnoitering on the off chance of turning the situation to their advantage, but when this seemed impossible they sailed away, while the home government disavowed the admiral's action and Rome accepted the apology, as recorded by Orosius. But whether Rome suspected treachery or merely rebuffed a friendly gesture, the result would hardly improve relations between the two Republics.

When King Pyrrhus left the shores of Sicily he is reported to have remarked: "What a cockpit we are now leaving for Carthaginian and Roman to fight in." And the recent history of the island justified this prophecy. The Punic expansion had been checked during the reign of Agathocles as King of Syracuse (304–289), but after his death the Carthaginians again advanced their standards, until driven back by Pyrrhus. When he retired to Italy they defeated the Syracusan fleet, recovered their lost possessions and reduced the Greek cities of central Sicily. Thus by 275 Syracuse's influence was confined to eastern Sicily, and even there she met with rivals. Certain of Agathocles' discharged Italian mercenaries on their return home had treacherously seized the town of Messana (c. 288). Styling themselves Mamertines, after the Sabellian war-god Mamers, they settled there and proceeded to plunder the surrounding districts, Carthaginian and Greek alike. Defeated but not exterminated by Pyrrhus, they were later attacked by the Syracusans under Hiero who profited by his victory to assume the title of king (265–264) and to undertake the siege of Messana. At this point the Carthaginians intervened, refusing to look on while Syracuse won control of the Sicilian straits by capturing Messana. Their admiral threw a Punic garrison into the town with the consent of the Mamertines, and Hiero perforce returned to Syracuse, disregarding the complimentary exhortations of the poet Theocritus to continue fighting. But the Mamertines did not wish to keep their new garrison indefinitely: some advocated reaching an agreement with Carthage by which their autonomy would be respected, others preferred to seek alliance with a less alien people, the Romans. The latter party prevailed and Rome was suddenly faced with a request for alliance and help. What was she to do?

Rome and Carthage were thus brought abruptly face to face. By ejecting from Rhegium the Campanians who had tried to play at pirates like the Mamertines in Sicily the Romans had won control of the Straits (270). But now a Carthaginian garrison at Messana faced them from the opposite shore: it barred their access to Sicily, and constituted a *point d'appui* whence, following the example set by Dionysius and Agathocles, the Carthaginians could sail against the towns of the Italian coast, when once they had reduced eastern Sicily. There could be no doubt that they would extend to Sicily the monopoly which they exercised throughout the western Mediterranean. That might not be of direct concern to the Romans, who were little interested in foreign trade, but it would be a severe blow to their allies in southern Italy. And there was the further danger that if Rome neglected her new Greek allies, they might turn to Carthage for protection in a desperate effort to preserve their Sicilian trade. It did indeed seem that Rome would have to listen to the appeal of the Mamertines, even though this might involve crossing swords with Carthage and possibly a deadly duel.

But the swords which the Mamertines virtually thrust into the rivals' hands could scarcely have been kept permanently sheathed. Rome and Carthage had little in common. Different in race, culture and religion, with divergent moral and material interests, they would gravitate towards conflict when once the minor states between them had been eliminated or assimilated. In the Hellenistic East a common culture held the three Great Monarchies in a precarious Balance of Powers. When Rome had absorbed something of that culture, she adapted her policy in order to try to maintain the balance. But in the west rivalry would conduce to war: compromise was difficult, if not impossible.

The immediate question before the Roman Senate was the appeal of the Mamertines, not war with Carthage, though the more far-sighted must have seen that this would probably follow the granting of the request. The Senate, however, could not reach a decision, so the People took the matter into their own hands and voted to send help to the Mamertines. Polybius, who here follows Fabius Pictor and thus gives at least a pro-Roman account, if not a tendencious justification, explains that the Senate hesitated, in spite of a full recognition of the danger of the advance of Carthage, because it felt unable to ally itself to a robber-state, especially as it had recently executed the brigands at Rhegium. But the weight of this moralistic argument has been questioned, since the seizure of Messana by the Mamertines had occurred twenty-five years earlier and the new state was now standing on its own feet and had been recognized by Carthage and several Greek cities; it was presumably autonomous and therefore Rome would not break her fetial law by granting alliance. Further, the parallel with Rhegium is weak, for there Rome interfered on behalf of her own allies, whereas she had had no dealings with Messana. But even if conscientious scruples were among the motives of the Senate's hesitation, others also must be found in the fear of war with a great sea power, and in the aversion of the conservative element in the Senate to an expansionist policy which increased the power of the People and of the popular leaders whom a new war might bring into prominence. A further reason was probably that Roman interference in Sicily would involve a definite breach of the treaty of 306. The democratic leaders who wanted war might argue that the Carthaginians had themselves annulled this agreement by their action at Tarentum, and by their recent aggressive behaviour which had stimulated Rhegium to ask Rome for protection (*c.* 280). But the Senators may have had some qualms about disregarding their formal obligations.

The People had accepted the Mamertine alliance because of the advantages which their leaders said would attend it. These suggested benefits would not be land, tribute, or even booty, but the checking of the advance of Carthage and the increase of allies with the consequent decrease of effort by the citizen army. The personal advantages to the democratic leaders from success in war was an aspect which they would hardly emphasize, but of which such families as the Otacilii of Beneventum and the Campanian Atilii would be fully conscious. But the main motive which led Rome to accept the alliance of the Mamertines was to secure an outpost which was necessary to the safety of Italy. The two rivals may both have rushed to secure this key position, but their motives were different; defensive imperialism dominated Rome's policy, an exploiting commercial imperialism actuated Carthage.

J. H. THIEL (b. 1896), professor of ancient history at the University of Utrecht, pulls no punches in his assertion of Rome's responsibility for the First Punic War. For Thiel, Rome overtly and consciously violated a long-standing treaty that forbade Roman intervention in Sicily, part of the Carthaginian sphere of influence. Furthermore, the Romans themselves, concerned with their image, made matters difficult for historians by falsifying the records in order to justify the imperialist venture in retrospect. Thiel's numerous works include *Studies on the History of Roman Sea-Power in Republican Times* and *A History of Roman Sea-Power before the Second Punic War.**

J. H. Thiel

Roman War Guilt

Polybius knows of three treaties concluded between Rome and Carthage, and he expressly states that there had been no more. Of these three treaties the last (P³) belongs without any doubt to the Pyrrhic war; ... P² must date from 348 and ... P¹ has to be assigned to the beginning of the republican era (the date given by Polybius) or at any rate to a date preceding 348. This means, that, if we follow Polybius, a treaty between Rome and Carthage was evidently *not* concluded in 306. On the other hand Livy mentions the conclusion of a Roman-Carthaginian treaty *sub anno* 306 (9, 43, 26), which he calls the third, and the treaty of the Pyrrhic war (P³) is consequently called by him the fourth (*perioch.* 13). In such a dilemma

there is usually a strong (and very often legitimate) tendency among scholars to prefer Polybius and to disavow Livy; but in this case there are very serious reasons to suppose that Polybius was wrong and that a treaty *was* concluded in 306. Livy does not specify the terms of this agreement: he simply states that a third treaty was concluded. But from other sources we know of certain terms of a Roman-Carthaginian agreement, which can only be the treaty of 306, and we derive this knowledge first of all ... from Polybius himself! For Polybius opposes strongly the opinion of the historian Philinus, who had asserted that there existed a treaty between Rome and Carthage, forbidding Roman intervention in Sicily and Carthaginian inter-

---

*From J. H. Thiel, *A History of Roman Sea-Power before the Second Punic War* (Amsterdam: North-Holland Publishing Company, 1954), pp. 12-15, 128-143. Footnotes omitted.

vention in Italy, and that therefore in 264 the Romans had violated the terms of this treaty by their intervention in Sicily which led to the first Punic war; in other words, Philinus had represented the Romans as the aggressors of 264, who had been found guilty of breach of faith. In an other source also we find traces of the existence of this treaty, which is so passionately denied by Polybius: Servius informs us (*ad Aen.* 4, 628) that there was an agreement *ut neque Romani ad litora Carthaginiensium accederent neque Carthaginienses ad litora Romanorum,* a stipulation which is, though in a somewhat vague way, in accordance with the terms of Philinus' treaty, and he adds that there was yet another stipulation *ut Corsica esset media inter Romanos et Carthaginienses,* in other words that there was a treaty forbidding Roman intervention in Sicily and Carthaginian intervention in Italy and allowing either party a free hand in Corsica as no man's land. Now P^1, P^2 and P^3 neither contain nor admit of such terms as mentioned by Philinus and Servius; so we may safely conclude that, *if* Philinus was right in asserting that such a treaty existed, it has to be identified with the treaty of 306. So the problem can be reduced to the question whether Philinus was right in vindicating the existence of such a treaty or Polybius in rejecting it. Now it is not true that, if we prefer Philinus' version, we implicitly regard Polybius as a perfidious liar and forger: Polybius may have acted in good faith, when he denied the existence of Philinus' treaty; but . . . he may have been imposed upon by his Roman informants. For Roman patriots had excellent reasons to juggle away the treaty of Philinus, because its very existence convicted the Romans of treaty-breaking and showed them up as the perfidious aggressors of 264. So we may well imagine a couple of Roman worthies simply suppressing the agreement of 306, showing Po-

lybius the three remaining treaties and telling him brazenly that there was nothing else. For the Romans were great masters both of patriotism and hypocrisy and the *fides Romana* was not better than the *fides Punica,* perhaps even worse: the Romans used to *speak* far too much of *fides,* which is a very bad sign. There is, however, yet another argument, and a very strong one, in favour of the existence of Philinus' treaty. The annalistic tradition is silent upon the treaty of 306 or rather upon its stipulations (Livy for instance informs us that in 306 a third treaty was concluded between Rome and Carthage, but he does not mention its terms); but nevertheless this same tradition presupposes the existence of the terms ascribed to it by Philinus. According to those annalists the Carthaginians sent a fleet to Tarentum in 272, when it was being besieged by the Romans, in order to help the Tarentines and, apparently, to gain a foothold (and a very strong one) in Italy; this endeavour came to nothing, because Pyrrhus' lieutenant, who had maintained the Tarentine citadel up to that moment, now surrendered it to the Romans, so that the Tarentines could no longer keep up resistance and had to surrender the city in their turn; so the Carthaginians sailed home again without having effected their purpose. In my opinion this story is a piece of annalistic forgery, and the reason for which it was forged is perfectly clear: its purport was to prove that several years before 264 the Carthaginians had already broken the treaty which they had concluded with Rome, and that therefore the Romans were no longer bound by it and were perfectly free to intervene in Sicily in 264, because Carthage had been the first to break the agreement. But it is equally clear that this piece of forgery, intended as it is to exculpate the Romans from the charge of breach of faith, presupposes the terms of Philinus' treaty, which forbade

Roman intervention in Sicily and Carthaginian intervention in Italy and which had been violated by the Romans in 264. . . .

It goes without saying that the first Punic war had a number of factual, objective causes which do not (and cannot) appear as matters involving *guilt:* it was caused by a certain combination of political and military forces, which in its turn was rooted in the historical development of the immediately preceding decades; this development gave Rome the command of the whole of Italy, also of Southern Italy, so that the Italian sphere of Rome and the Sicilian sphere of Carthage became dangerously contiguous and the centuries-old friendship between the two powers, which had never been very warm, now cooled off. It stands to reason that this situation reached a very critical stage when Carthage occupied Messana: the great naval power of Carthage was now in control of one side of the Straits (Messana), Rome of the other (Rhegium). As far as Rome was concerned, Carthage had every right to occupy the city of the Mamertines: she did not break a treaty by doing so. But on the other hand it would be unreasonable to deny that Rome had good reason to regard this occupation as a thorn in her flesh.

All this is quite true: the Romans *had* reasons of their own to expel the Punic garrison from Messana and to put a Roman garrison into the city. But this does not alter the fact that by doing so Rome broke a treaty and that on the other hand the Carthaginians did all they could to prevent a conflict; which means that Rome was the aggressor, and that the guilt of causing the war was on the Roman side and on the Roman side alone: Rome had *reason* to throw the Carthaginians out of Messana, but she had *no right* to do it, which makes all the difference from a mor-

al point of view. There is a tendency among historians to regard problems of war-guilt as quite negligible; in my eyes this is an unworthy attitude. It is not the task of the historian to gloss over crimes and to regard power and success as the only standards by which he is to judge human conduct in the past. Scoundrels are scoundrels and treaty-breakers are treaty-breakers: it does not make the least difference whether a crime was committed and a treaty treacherously broken more than 2000 years ago or yesterday. The treaty concluded between Rome and Carthage in 306 forbade Punic intervention in Italy and Roman intervention in Sicily: the Romans broke this treaty by occupying Messana in 264. Why extenuate such a flagrant violation of *fides*? Because poor little Rome was such a dear and because the Romans are our great spiritual ancestors? Or because the Carthaginians were no more than despicable "hucksters" and "shopkeepers" who deserved what was coming to them? The truth is that in 264 the Carthaginians behaved like somewhat weak gentlemen, the Romans on the contrary like rogues, and hypocritical rogues into the bargain; is it the historian's duty to speak the truth or to obscure it? In 264 dear good old little Rome was simply hitting below the belt, while affecting the expression of an injured innocent.

Am I committing a bad anachronism by applying a modern standard to ancient Roman war practice? Modern indeed! The Romans knew quite well that by occupying Messana in 264 they violated their own principle of non-aggression: if not, the Roman historians would not have tampered with the treaty of 306 as they did. Of course Roman historiography found it hard to swallow the treaty of 306; for Rome never violated a treaty and never committed an act of aggression: she only defended herself. So it was necessary to resort to lies and forgeries, in order to reconcile the ignoble practice of warfare with the noble theory; but . . . Roman historical tradition did not stick consistently to one lie, but followed two different ways. The older remedy consisted in spiriting away the treaty of 306 and denying its existence: it was in good faith that Polybius fell for this trick, when he tried to investigate these matters at Rome. But the younger annalists chose another way: they did not deny the existence of the treaty, but forged a case of Punic intervention in Italy before 264, so that according to them Carthage had been the first to break the treaty and consequently Rome was no longer bound by it in 264. The two methods of lying refute one another: the fact that the older method tried to deny and obscure the existence of the treaty proves that the Punic attempt at intervention in Italy before 264 as handed down to us by younger annalists must be a forgery; for why attempt to deny the existence of the treaty, if Carthage had really been the first to break it? And this forgery committed by younger annalists proves in its turn that the older attempt to deny the existence of the treaty had been a fraud; for the said forgery is based on the terms of that treaty and presupposes its existence. If Roman historiography had adopted one consistent system of lying in this case, it would hardly have been possible for us to hunt down the truth; but, since two lies were put forth which are mutually exclusive, it *is* possible to reconstruct the truth by means of these very lies; the problem of war-guilt has to be decided in favour of Carthage.

Had the Romans a right to regard the treaty of 306 as superannuated in 264, because it had been concluded 42 years before, and could they reasonably believe themselves to be freed from the obligations imposed upon them by its terms, because it was to be regarded as antiquated? Certainly not. For one thing it is quite improbable that the treaty of 306 should have been concluded for a limited number of years (say 40), so that the term of its validity should have expired before 264: if so, the Romans would not have found it necessary to deny the existence of the treaty, which was what they did. Moreover, the period which separated the third from the second treaty (348–306) amounted to exactly the same number of years as that between the third treaty (306) and 264, and the period between the first and second treaties (508–348) had numbered as many as 160 years! In spite of such long periods peace had always been maintained between Carthage and Rome on the strength of those treaties. In the third place, the *symmachia* concluded between Rome and Carthage in 278 against Pyrrhus was no more than a special military clause added to the treaty of 306, which means that as late as 278 the treaty of 306 was still alive in the eyes of both Rome and Carthage. It is doubtless true that the military alliance of 278 yielded no practical results on account of a steadily growing mutual suspicion which had already been present when the alliance was concluded, and that this alliance automatically came to an end together with the war against Pyrrhus; but this does not mean that the treaty of 306 should have expired together with the temporary military agreement. It is also true that, contrary to the terms of the military alliance, the Carthaginians tried to effect a separate agreement with Pyrrhus during his operations in Sicily: if they had succeeded in concluding such a separate peace with Pyrrhus, they would have broken and therefore abolished the military agreement with Rome, but they would neither have broken nor invalidated the treaty of 306; moreover . . . the separate agreement with Pyrrhus was not effected. The friendly relations between Rome and

Carthage were certainly strained by occurrences like this: the fact that Rome appealed to Hiero for naval support against Rhegium in 270 and not to Carthage, was doubtless the Roman answer—and a not unreasonable answer—to the preceding Carthaginian attempt at disloyalty. But such an *attempt* on the part of Carthage did not justify a flagrant breach of treaty and a brutal act of aggression on the part of Rome in 264: it is worthy of note that, as far as we know, Rome did not appeal to the Punic attempt to conclude a separate peace with Pyrrhus in order to vindicate her own line of conduct in 264. That such a justification was regarded as far too weak—which, indeed, it was—is proved by the fact that a Punic attempt at intervention in Italy in 272 was invented in order to justify the Roman act of aggression of 264.

It is only reasonable to admit that the terms of the treaty of 306, which had been in perfect harmony with the political situation of that age, when Rome was no more than a humble state in Central Italy, which was still fighting the Samnites and which, though it *had* certain aspirations to control Southern Italy, had certainly no aspirations at all in the direction of Sicily, no longer fitted the situation in the sixties of the third century, after Rome had mastered the whole of Italy, including Rhegium. Without any doubt the Romans had serious reasons to regard the appearance of Carthage on the Straits as utterly unpleasant from their own point of view. From now on Messana constituted a Punic bridge-head whence, following the example set by Dionysius and Agathocles, the Carthaginians could sail against the towns of the Italian coast, when once they had reduced eastern Sicily. There could be little doubt that after reducing eastern Sicily they would extend to Sicily the monopoly which they exercised throughout the western Mediterranean and which Rome had acknowledged in her treaties with Carthage. That might not be of direct concern to the Romans themselves, who were little interested in foreign trade, but it would be a severe blow to their allies in Southern Italy. And there was the further danger that if Rome neglected the interests of her new Greek allies, they might turn to Carthage for protection in a desperate effort to preserve their Sicilian trade. Even before reducing eastern Sicily Carthage could blockade the Straits and prevent Neapolitan and other merchantmen from passing through in the direction of Syracuse. In a word, Rome had not only to regard Punic Messana as a potential military menace in the direction of Southern Italy, but she was also responsible for the economic well-being of her allies in that part of Italy, which was threatened just as well by the presence of Punic forces in Messana.

So it was only reasonable that in 267 the Romans should create a new (auxiliary) naval organization in order to protect the Italian coasts somewhat more efficiently than before: partially at least this reorganization may have been the Roman answer to the Punic occupation of Messana in 269 or 268, and it stands to reason that Rome had every right in the world to protect her own interests in this way. And it would have been quite reasonable again if, when in 264 the Mamertines implored the protection of the Romans against Carthage, they had used this request as a means to put pressure on Carthage, instead of simply accepting the Mamertines and committing a treacherous act of aggression without any warning: they might have warned Carthage that, if she did not agree to evacuate Messana, public opinion in Roman Italy might compel them to accept the Mamertines and to resort to force, and they might have asked for the addition of a clause to the treaty of 306 forbidding Carthage to occupy Messana. It is easy to remark that the Carthaginians would only have laughed at such demands, but it is quite gratuitous too: we cannot know what the result would have been, but we do know that, far from wanting a conflict with Rome in 264, Carthage did all she could to prevent it. And in any case, if the Romans had begun a war against Carthage after a vain but serious attempt at bringing the obsolete treaty of 306 up to date by peaceful means, they would have been far more justified than they were. For now they simply tore up that treaty as if it were a scrap of paper, and thus made knaves of themselves according to their own standards. In a word, the Roman aims of 264 were rather legitimate, but the means used were thoroughly damnable.

One may remark that, if the Romans had not surprised the Punic garrison, bullied it out of Messana and garrisoned the town themselves before a Punic fleet could reach the harbour, they would never have been able to occupy Messana in 264; that therefore they did not attempt negotiations with the government of Carthage, but preferred to break the treaty of 306 treacherously and without any previous negotiation or warning. There *is* something in that, but it does not shake my position: it only tends to prove that the Roman line of conduct in 264 was a purely Machiavellian one, that they deliberately broke the treaty of 306 without any warning, because they regarded such a method as profitable, *i.e.* because they knew that the first blow is half the battle. It is; but it is just the same thing to say that successful crime is the art of the unexpected: the Romans did behave like rogues, and that is just what I wanted to demonstrate.

In conclusion we have to pay attention to the deliberations in the senate and the assembly at Rome in connexion with the Mamertine request.

Messana had been occupied by Carthage in 269 or 268 in order to save the Mamertine community from destruction by Syracuse and, naturally, to give Carthage a bridge-head on the Straits. The Punic garrison had continued to hold the city until 264, but the Mamertines had gradually got tired of it, because, being born brigands, they did not like the peaceful way of life imposed upon them by Carthage. So a Mamertine embassy was sent to Rome in 264 in order to ask for protection against Carthage: they offered to surrender their city to Rome and begged for military assistance as a kindred people.

First of all it must be emphasized that the Mamertine request took the form of what the Romans called a *deditio*: Polybius' words (*urbem dedebant*: they offered to surrender the city; note the conative part. impf.) prove this conclusively and the fact that afterwards during negotiations with the Carthaginians and Hiero who were besieging Messana the principal argument used by the Romans turned on their *fides* points in just the same direction: in *fidem venire, in fidem accipi* is simply identical with *deditio*. In my opinion this fact is essential to our understanding of the Roman attitude with respect to the Mamertine request, and it is far too often ignored or insufficiently taken into account by those who write about the Roman decision of 264.

A second item of importance is the fact—for I regard it as a fact—that the Roman senate, when confronted with the Mamertine request, hesitated and could not reach a decision. What were the reasons for this hesitation? There were certainly reasons enough. On the one hand there must have been a number of honourable, strictly conscientious men in the senate who were not likely to break lightheartedly the treaty that forbade Roman intervention in Sicily; there must have been others who, though not being very particular about breach of faith, if vital interests were at stake, were fully aware that the acceptance of the Mamertines as allies would probably result in a great military conflict with Carthage which they did not want to start, and who in a more general way were apprehensive of the incalculable consequences of an aggressive policy of expansion outside Italy (Paul Meyer, 41–42: Polybius does not mention this argument, but see Zonar. 8, 8, 1); thirdly, the Mamertines were robbers and criminals who had mastered Messana in a brutal and illegitimate way and they had been the allies of the brigands at Rhegium who had recently been put to death by Rome, so that many a senator may have felt uneasy about allying themselves to such a robber-community. On the other hand there must have been senators with whom the risk of Punic intervention in Southern Italy, which was inherent in a permanent occupation of Messana by Carthage, and the damage to the commercial interests of the Italiot cities that might also result from it, weighed more heavily than the sanctity of treaties; part of them may even have sympathized with the Mamertines, because they were their kinsmen, or cherished secret imperialistic designs which went far beyond a simple occupation of Messana, or both: think of the Atilii from Campania and the Otacilii from Samnium who were kinsmen of the Oscan Mamertines and who, quite apart from sympathizing with them, had a better understanding and feeling for the economic interests of Southern Italy and, may be, were also

more interested in naval matters on account of their origin than the old aboriginal Roman aristocracy; think also of the Valerii of 263 and 261, who, together with the Otacilii who were their colleagues, were the principal promoters of a strong naval policy, without which Sicily could never be completely conquered: they may have been imperialists from the start, and in any case they must have been fervent supporters of an alliance with Messana. Nor must we forget that both the Atilii and the Otacilii were allied to the old Roman *gens Fabia,* and that Appius Claudius Caudex, the consul of 264 who brought the difficult problem of the Mamertine alliance before the people, was a kinsman of Appius Claudius Caecus, the great censor: certain imperialistic tendencies may have been present in him too. That is as may be; but, whether or not there were certain imperialistic elements in the Roman senate from the very start—this remains uncertain—, it will be perfectly clear that there were reasons in plenty—and important enough—on either side to bring about a kind of fifty-fifty balance in the senate; so the decision was left to the *comitia.* . . .

So we have to ask: what induced a not inconsiderable number of Roman peasants to accept the *deditio* of the Mamertines? Polybius' account is rather confused and weak on this essential point. He says that the commons, exhausted as they were by the preceding wars and in need of every kind of relief, decided to help the Mamertines, because the consuls (read *consul, v.s.*), besides emphasizing that the interest of the Roman community was at stake, promised them great individual profit in the way of plunder. Apart from the interest of the community . . . this story has not a leg to stand on: the peasants, worn out as they were by recent wars, . . . wanted a new war because of the plunder it would

ve them! This is really too absurd: if the
oman peasants were exhausted by recent
ars—and they certainly were—, they
anted rest, they wanted to be left alone,
 order to be able to till the soil and to go
out their own business, and in any case
ere was one thing they did not want: a
w war, and a war outside Italy at that!
Caudex had really tried to win the peas-
ts over in such a simple way, his propos-
would have been rejected. So the ques-
n remains to be answered: what did in-
ce a considerable number of peasants to
cept it? . . .

A *deditio* offered by suppliants who
mbly implored the protection of Rome
as not taken casually by the Romans:
ey regarded their *fides* as strongly in-
lved in such a situation. The most elabo-
te account of such a *deditio* which we pos-
ss, that of the Campanian *deditio* in 343,
perhaps a rather artificial and therefore
t quite reliable construction; but, if it is
fabrication, it has at any rate been fabri-
ted by a Roman and therefore it reflects
oman sentiment, in spite of incorrect le-
l technicalities. It proves that the Ro-
ans found it very hard to reject such a
quest, that there was at least a tendency
nong them in such a case to regard their
es as almost engaged in advance. Of
urse the Romans had a right to reject
ch a *deditio*, and it was even their duty to
 so, if the acceptance of the *deditio* im-
ied violation of an existing treaty; but for
 that the Romans considered such a situ-
ion as tragic, because *fides* conflicted
th *fides*. It is hardly correct to say that, if
e Romans rejected an offer of *deditio* and
thereupon the suppliants simply surren-
red themselves, Rome had no choice but
 accept the *fait accompli*. But the fact that
omans could think of putting it that way
oves that the atmosphere of *deditio* was
ghly charged with the electricity of senti-

ment and moral obligation and that in
such cases the Romans regarded their *fides*
as strongly engaged.

In a word, the Mamertine offer of *deditio*
presented the consul with a fine opportunity to display samples of sophistical dema-
gogy which promised a striking success.
He could say that the Romans had always
regarded it as a moral duty to accept suppliants in distress who offered to surrender
themselves; and such a remark would be
all the more impressive, because the Romans did in fact take cases like this very
seriously. He could say that, if the assembly turned down the Mamertine request and if the Mamertines then simply
surrendered themselves instead of *offering*
to do so, the assembly would have to accept the accomplished fact, because their
fides would be irrevocably engaged; so why
not accept the Mamertines at once, before
the accomplished fact was forced upon
them in humiliating circumstances? In a
word, he could follow the same lines of rea-
soning as Livius (or rather his predecessor)
followed in describing the *deditio* of the
Campanians. He could say: 'Citizens, this
is a tragic situation: *fides* stands against
fides, and so you have to choose between
two evils. If you accept the Mamertines,
you will break the treaty of 306; if you
stick to that treaty and reject the Mamertine request, you will not have kept
faith with suppliants who want to surrender themselves. You *have* to choose between
these two painful alternatives, and you are
perfectly free to choose between them, but
I request you urgently to choose the lesser
of the two evils. Citizens, the choice is
yours!' Of course this would have been no
more than sophistical casuistry: it is evident that the treaty of 306 took precedence
of the Mamertine request because of its
priority. But, if the consul stated the case
in such a way as I have supposed, if he

deliberately and adroitly confused and beclouded the issue, which alternative would appeal to the Roman peasants or at any rate to a considerable number of them, to those who were simple, primitive men? Would they cling to the treaty of 306, which was remote and abstract in their eyes and which had been concluded with people who could no longer be regarded as real friends in the present situation? Or would they accept the Mamertine *deditio* which was of the present, concrete and tangible, and which appealed directly to their Roman feelings? It is not difficult to give the answer....

Moreover, the peasants who had voted affirmatively, had done so because they wanted to free Messana and not because they wanted to start a great war against Carthage: it was the last thing they had bargained for and the consul had certainly not warned them that the probability of such a war was great, if they accepted his proposal. So these elements also were apt to demur—although they got what they deserved—when Roman intervention in

Sicily resulted in a great, lingering war, a the more so because it brought grievou hardship to Italy.

I may add that even those who in 26 really wanted a war against Carthage— they can hardly have been numerous— could not foresee the character and dura tion of the war they were about to unleash if in 264 the Romans had had an inklin of the ordeals which the immediate futur had in store for them, it is possible that no a single man would have voted for Cau dex' proposal. Men can desire fervently t start a war and all the same get tired of and dispirited, if the war proves to be ver costly in lives and money, and almost in terminable. It is much more remarkabl that the Romans succeeded in keeping th disappointment and despair in their ran within reasonable limits and in adherin firmly to their war-purpose than that ther *was* a certain amount of demoralizatio and despair among them: remarkabl and—let us give them their due—ad mirable.

M. CARY (1881–1958), for many years professor of ancient history at the University of London, was one of the most versatile and accomplished students of antiquity. Many books and articles on both Greek and Roman history stand to his credit. His editorship of the standard Methuen series on the "History of the Greek and Roman World" is sufficient testimony to the breadth of his interest. Cary contributed the volume on Hellenistic Greece to that series. His *History of Rome* has been perhaps the most successful one-volume treatment of the subject. In this selection, he sees the initial conflict between Rome and Carthage as one into which both parties drifted irresponsibly, and he eschews the notion of an inevitable clash.*

M. Cary

An Accidental War

The Carthaginian government was an oligarchy of wealthy merchants, which has been aptly compared with the aristocracy of medieval Venice. The effective organs of administration were a senate with an inner council of thirty leading nobles, and a high court of one hundred judges, also drawn from the ruling families. The aristocracy humoured the commons to the extent of consulting them on highly important or debatable questions, of buying from them the principal offices of state, and of leaving their hands the petty charges and perquisites. At the same time it kept a jealous eye on its professional generals, and took ample precautions against attempts at military revolutions.

In its foreign relations the Punic government pursued the same tenacious but cautious policy by which the Venetian republic built up its empire. Though it never scrupled, if necessary, to defend its mercantile interests by force of arms, it none the less avoided war where peaceful methods availed, and it never resorted to hostilities without some definite gain in view. In Africa it annexed no more than a portion of Tunisia and Tripoli, embracing in all some 20,000 square miles. In its relations with the Italian states (where its trade connexions were not extensive) it relied upon diplomacy to remove in advance the causes of a possible clash. In the sixth century it had come to amicable

*From M. Cary, *A History of Rome Down to the Reign of Constantine* (London: Macmillan & Co. Ltd., 1954), pp. 143–145. Reprinted by permission of Macmillan & Co., Ltd., London, The Macmillan Company of Canada, Ltd., and St. Martin's Press, Inc. Footnotes omitted.

terms with the Etruscan seaboard towns. In the fourth century, as soon as the Romans acquired an extensive sea-front along the Latin coast, it offered them two successive treaties. . . . In 279 it supplemented these pacts with a military alliance against Pyrrhus, and although neither party actually gave armed support to the other, it is not unlikely that the Romans drew a subsidy in money from their confederates. . . .

In spite of these friendly overtures, the Romans harboured a suspicion that the Carthaginians might seek to control the Italian coasts in the same manner as they dominated the seaboard of Spain and Sicily. In each of their three treaties they had stipulated that the Carthaginians must not take any permanent foothold on Italian soil. Between 350 and 270 they had established a chain of coastguard colonies, composed of Romans without any admixture of Latins, from Etruria to Campania. In 311 they had commissioned a flotilla of cruisers to patrol the Italian coast, and in 267 they had specially charged the new *quaestores Italici* or *classici* with the supervision of naval defences. Nevertheless as late as 264 a clash between Rome and Carthage was nothing more than a remote contingency. It required a very peculiar concatenation of aggravating circumstances to bring about the First Punic War.

By a not unnatural yet fatal oversight, no attempt had been made in the aforementioned treaties to define exactly the respective spheres of the contracting parties in Sicily, where the Romans as yet had no important interest, political or commercial. Because of this gap in the covenant, an unforeseen situation arose at Messana, a city whose commanding position on the straits that carry its name had made it into a long-standing object of contention between Carthaginians and Greeks. In 264 Messana was suddenly

thrown into the political market. Since 28[?] it had been in the hands of a corps of dis-charged Campanian mercenaries, wh[?] went by the name of "Mamertines" (sor[?] of Mars). Twenty-five years later it wa[?] put under siege by king Hiero of Syracus[?] the most powerful of the remaining Gree[?] states on the island. The capture of Me[?]sana by Hiero would probably have e[?]tailed the wholesale execution of the garr[?]son, for the Mamertines were no bett[?] than a Grand Catalan Company wh[?] lived by systematically plundering [?] blackmailing the rest of Sicily. In this e[?]tremity the Mamertines accepted an off[?] of help from an expectant Punic flotill[?] whose admiral thereupon induced Hiero [?] call off his attack. But as soon as they we[?] rid of Hiero, they cast about for means [?] ushering out their Carthaginian guest, wh[?] was outstaying his welcome, and resolve[?] to offer themselves as allies to the Roman[?] upon whom they could make a claim [?] the ground of common race. In extricati[?] themselves from their scrape, the Campa[?]nian adventurers contrived to set Roma[?] and Carthaginians by the ears.

The appeal of the Mamertines raise[?] substantially the same issue at Rome [?] the call for help from the Campanians [?] Capua in 343. . . . Were they to assum[?] new and possibly indefinite obligations [?] taking sides in a dispute that did not co[?]cern them directly? On the one hand, th[?] acquisition of Messana by the Carthagi[?]ians would furnish them with a potenti[?] base of attack upon Italy, and their pre[?]ence in that city could not be simply i[?]nored. On the other, to say nothing of th[?] disreputable character of the appellants, [?] was to be feared that a Roman interve[?]tion in Sicily might be resented by th[?] Carthaginians as a trespass upon their pr[?]serves, and thus might lead on to a war f[?] which there was otherwise no clear wa[?]rant. In the Senate opinions were so even[?]

balanced that it weakly referred the matter to the Comitia without any positive recommendation. The voters in the popular assembly, who still felt the need of rest after the great effort of the Pyrrhic war, showed equal hesitation at first, but were eventually won over to action by the presiding consuls, who represented to the commons that an expedition to Sicily might bring in large "benefits", *i.e.* military reputations for the commanders and booty for the troops. The Comitia, it is true, at first went no further than to order a relief expedition to Messana, and the Roman detachment which was sent to carry out these instructions fulfilled them without any shedding of blood, for the Punic commander lost his nerve at the unexpected appearance of the Romans and tamely withdrew from the city. But the Carthaginian government had no intention of being bluffed in this fashion out of its claims upon Messana. It forthwith sent an expeditionary force to recover the lost prize, and it succeeded in bringing Hiero back into the field, this time against the Roman interlopers. On the other hand the Senate reinforced the small corps of occupation with a consular army. Thus the scuffle round Messana drew on the Romans and Carthaginians into formal war.

For this drift into hostilities both parties may be considered equally responsible. Had either of them, instead of attempting to steal a march upon the other, made an offer of fresh negotiations, a durable compromise should not have been difficult to arrange. An agreement by which the Carthaginians kept Messana but conceded the freedom of the Straits to Rome and Syracuse and their allies might have offered a fair basis for a lasting peace. On the other hand, both parties may be acquitted of using the affair of Messana as a pretext for a predetermined war. The collision which brought on the First Punic War was wholly accidental.

The towering intellect of THEODOR MOMMSEN (1817–1903) dwarfs by comparison all others who have ever engaged in the study of the Roman world. A giant among his contemporaries, Mommsen's stature continues to grow with the lengthening list of scholars who find themselves continually in his debt. His teaching career, at Leipzig, Zurich, Breslau, and Berlin, spanned more than half a century. It was at Berlin from 1858 until the end of his life that his learning and productivity earned him an unrivaled international reputation climaxed by the Nobel Prize for Literature in 1902. No Roman historian has ever combined Mommsen's unerring mastery of detail with the power and sweep of his conception. His monumental works on Roman law and the Roman constitution and his collection and editing of the entire corpus of Latin inscriptions are permanent and indispensable contributions. The selection here is from Mommsen's *History of Rome,* which contains some of his most influential judgments and his most forceful writing. He propounds a favorable verdict on Rome's philhellenic sympathies in her eastern policy.*

Theodor Mommsen

Philhellenism

When Philip concluded his treaty with the Aetolians and Romans in 205, he seriously intended to make a lasting peace with Rome, and to devote himself exclusively in future to the affairs of the east. It admits of no doubt that he saw with regret the rapid subjugation of Carthage; and it may be, that Hannibal hoped for a second declaration of war from Macedonia, and that Philip secretly reinforced the last Carthaginian army with mercenaries. . . . But the tedious affairs in which he had meanwhile involved himself in the east, as

well as the nature of the alleged support, and especially the total silence of the Romans as to such a breach of the peace while they were searching for grounds of war, place it beyond doubt, that Philip was by no means disposed in 203 to make up for what he ought to have done ten years before.

He had turned his eyes to an entirely different quarter. Ptolemy Philopator of Egypt had died in 205. Philip and Antiochus, the kings of Macedonia and Asia, had combined against his successor Ptol-

*From Theodor Mommsen, *The History of Rome,* translated by W. P. Dickson (New York, 1895), vol. II, pp. 409–419, 435–437, 441–443. Footnotes omitted.

emy Epiphanes, a child of five years old, in order completely to gratify the ancient grudge which the monarchies of the mainland entertained towards the maritime state. The Egyptian state was to be broken up; Egypt and Cyprus were to fall to Antiochus; Cyrene, Ionia, and the Cyclades to Philip. Thoroughly after the manner of Philip, who ridiculed such considerations, the kings began the war not merely without cause, but even without pretext, "just as the large fishes devour the small." The allies, moreover, had made their calculations correctly, especially Philip. Egypt had enough to do in defending herself against the nearer enemy in Syria, and was obliged to leave her possessions in Asia Minor and the Cyclades undefended when Philip threw himself upon these as his share of the spoil. . . .

But even had this not been so, the interests of all Greek commercial cities were at stake. They could not possibly allow the mild and almost purely nominal Egyptian rule to be supplanted by the Macedonian despotism, with which urban self-government and freedom of commercial intercourse were not at all compatible; and the fearful treatment of the Cians showed that the matter at stake was not the right of confirming the charters of the towns, but the life or death of one and all. Lampsacus had already fallen, and Thasos had been treated like Cius; no time was to be lost. Theophiliscus, the vigilant *strategus* of Rhodes, exhorted his citizens to meet the common danger by common resistance, and not to suffer the towns and islands to become one by one a prey to the enemy. Rhodes resolved on its course, and declared war against Philip. Byzantium joined it; as did also the aged Attalus king of Pergamus, personally and politically the enemy of Philip. . . .

In fact a storm was gathering against Philip in the west, which did not permit him to continue the plundering of defenceless Egypt. The Romans, who had at length in this year concluded peace on their own terms with Carthage, began to give serious attention to these complications in the east. It has often been affirmed, that after the conquest of the west they forthwith proceeded to the subjugation of the east; a serious consideration will lead to a juster judgment. It is only dull prejudice which fails to see that Rome at this period by no means grasped at the sovereignty of the Mediterranean states, but, on the contrary, desired nothing further than to have neighbours that should not be dangerous in Africa and in Greece; and Macedonia was not really dangerous to Rome. Its power certainly was far from small, and it is evident that the Roman senate only consented with reluctance to the peace of 205, which left it in all its integrity; but how little any serious apprehensions of Macedonia were or could be entertained in Rome, is best shown by the small number of troops— who yet were never compelled to fight against a superior force—with which Rome carried on the next war. The senate doubtless would have gladly seen Macedonia humbled; but that humiliation would be too dearly purchased at the cost of a land war carried on in Macedonia with Roman troops; and accordingly, after the withdrawal of the Aetolians, the senate voluntarily concluded peace at once on the basis of the *status quo*. It is therefore far from made out, that the Roman government concluded this peace with the definite design of beginning the war at a more convenient season; and it is very certain that, at the moment, from the thorough exhaustion of the state and the extreme unwillingness of the citizens to enter into a second transmarine struggle, the Macedonian war was in a high degree unwelcome to the Romans. But now it was inevitable.

They might have acquiesced in the Macedonian state as a neighbour, such as it stood in 205; but it was impossible that they could permit it to acquire the best part of Asiatic Greece and the important Cyrene, to crush the neutral commercial states, and thereby to double its power. Further, the fall of Egypt and the humiliation, perhaps the subjugation, of Rhodes would have inflicted deep wounds on the trade of Sicily and Italy; and could Rome remain a quiet spectator, while Italian commerce with the east was made dependent on the two great continental powers? Rome had, moreover, an obligation of honour to fulfil towards Attalus her faithful ally since the first Macedonian war, and had to prevent Philip, who had already besieged him in his capital, from expelling him from his dominions. Lastly, the claim of Rome to extend her protecting arm over all the Hellenes was by no means an empty phrase: the citizens of Neapolis, Rhegium, Massilia, and Emporiae could testify that that protection was meant in earnest, and there is no question at all that at this time the Romans stood in a closer relation to the Greeks than any other nation—one little more remote than that of the Hellenized Macedonians. It is strange that any should dispute the right of the Romans to feel their human, as well as their Hellenic, sympathies revolted at the outrageous treatment of the Cians and Thasians.

Thus in reality all political, commercial, and moral motives concurred in inducing Rome to undertake the second war against Philip—one of the most righteous, which the city ever waged. It greatly redounds to the honour of the senate, that it immediately resolved on its course and did not allow itself to be deterred from making the necessary preparations either by the exhaustion of the state or by the unpopularity of such a declaration of war. The propraetor

Marcus Valerius Laevinus made his appearance as early as 201 with the Sicilian fleet of 38 sail in the eastern waters. The government, however, were at a loss to discover an ostensible pretext for the war; a pretext which they needed in order to satisfy the people, even although they had not been far too sagacious to undervalue, as was the manner of Philip, the importance of assigning a legitimate ground for hostilities. The support, which Philip was alleged to have granted to the Carthaginians after the peace with Rome, manifestly could not be proved. The Roman subjects, indeed, in the province of Illyria had for a considerable time complained of the Macedonian encroachments. In 203 a Roman envoy at the head of the Illyrian levy had driven Philip's troops from the Illyrian territory; and the senate had accordingly declared to the king's envoys in 202, that if he sought war, he would find it sooner than was agreeable to him. But these encroachments were simply the ordinary outrages which Philip practised towards his neighbours; a negotiation regarding them at the present moment would have led to his humbling himself and offering satisfaction, but not to war. With all the belligerent powers in the east the Roman community was nominally in friendly relations, and might have granted them aid in repelling Philip's attack. But Rhodes and Pergamus, which naturally did not fail to request Roman aid, were formally the aggressors; and although Alexandrian ambassadors besought the Roman senate to undertake the guardianship of the boy king, Egypt appears to have been by no means eager to invoke the direct intervention of the Romans, which would put an end to her difficulties for the moment, but would at the same time open up the eastern sea to the great western power. Aid to Egypt, moreover, must have been in the first instance rendered in Syria, and would have entangled Rome simultaneously in a war with Asia and with Macedonia; which the Romans were naturally the more desirous to avoid, as they were firmly resolved not to intermeddle at least in Asiatic affairs. No course was left but to despatch in the meantime an embassy to the east for the purpose, first, of obtaining—what was not in the circumstances difficult—the sanction of Egypt to the interference of the Romans in the affairs of Greece; secondly, of pacifying king Antiochus by abandoning Syria to him; and, lastly, of accelerating as much as possible a breach with Philip and promoting a coalition of the minor Graeco-Asiatic states against him (end of 201). At Alexandria they had no difficulty in accomplishing their object; the court had no choice, and was obliged gratefully to receive Marcus Aemilius Lepidus, whom the senate had despatched as "guardian of the king" to uphold his interests, so far as that could be done without an actual intervention. Antiochus did not break off his alliance with Philip, nor did he give to the Romans the definite explanations which they desired; in other respects, however—whether from remissness, or influenced by the declarations of the Romans that they did not wish to interfere in Syria—he pursued his schemes in that direction and left things in Greece and Asia Minor to take their course. . . .

Meanwhile, however, the occasion for declaring war, which Rome desired, had been furnished from another quarter. The Athenians in their silly and cruel vanity had put to death two unfortunate Acarnanians, because these had accidentally strayed into their mysteries. When the Acarnanians, who were naturally indignant, asked Philip to procure them satisfaction, he could not refuse the just request of his most faithful allies, and he allowed them to levy men in Macedonia and, with these

and their own troops, to invade Attica without a formal declaration of war. This, it is true, was no war in the proper sense of the term; and, besides, the leader of the Macedonian band, Nicanor, immediately gave orders to his troops to retreat, when the Roman envoys, who were at Athens at the time, used threatening language (in the end of 201). But it was too late. An Athenian embassy was sent to Rome to report the attack made by Philip on an ancient ally of the Romans; and, from the way in which the senate received it, Philip saw clearly what awaited him; so that he at once, in the very spring of 200, directed Philocles, his general in Greece, to lay waste the Attic territory and to reduce the city to extremities.

The senate now had what they wanted; and in the summer of 200 they were able to propose to the comitia a declaration of war "on account of an attack on a state in alliance with Rome.". . .

It was completely in the power of the Romans to dictate peace; they used their power without abusing it. The empire of Alexander might be annihilated; at a conference of the allies this desire was expressly put forward by the Aetolians. But what else would this mean, than to demolish the rampart protecting Hellenic culture from the Thracians and Celts? Already during the war just ended the flourishing Lysimachia on the Thracian Chersonese had been totally destroyed by the Thracians—a serious warning for the future. Flamininus, who had clearly perceived the bitter animosities subsisting among the Greek states, could never consent that the great Roman power should be the executioner for the grudges of the Aetolian confederacy, even if his Hellenic sympathies had not been as much won by the polished and chivalrous king as his Roman national feeling was offended by the boastings of the

Aetolians, the "victors of Cynoscephalae," as they called themselves. He replied to the Aetolians that it was not the custom of Rome to annihilate the vanquished, and that, besides, they were their own masters and were at liberty to put an end to Macedonia, if they could. The king was treated with all possible deference, and, on his declaring himself ready now to entertain the demands formerly made, an armistice for a considerable term was agreed to by Flamininus in return for the payment of a sum of money and the furnishing of hostages, among whom was the king's son Demetrius,—an armistice which Philip greatly needed in order to expel the Dardani out of Macedonia.

The final regulation of the complicated affairs of Greece was entrusted by the senate to a commission of ten persons, the head and soul of which was Flamininus. Philip obtained from it terms similar to those laid down for Carthage. He lost all his foreign possessions in Asia Minor, Thrace, Greece, and in the islands of the Aegean Sea; while he retained Macedonia proper undiminished, with the exception of some unimportant tracts on the frontier and the province of Orestis, which was declared free—a stipulation which Philip felt very keenly, but which the Romans could not avoid prescribing, for with his character it was impossible to leave him free to dispose of subjects who had once revolted from their allegiance. Macedonia was further bound not to conclude any foreign alliances without the previous knowledge of Rome, and not to send garrisons abroad; she was bound, moreover, not to make war out of Macedonia against civilized states or against any allies of Rome at all; and she was not to maintain any army exceeding 5000 men, any elephants, or more than five decked ships—the rest were to be given up to the Romans. Lastly, Philip entered into symmachy with the Romans, which obliged him to send a contingent when requested; indeed, Macedonian troops immediately afterwards fought side by side with the legions. Moreover, he paid a contribution of 1000 talents (£244,000).

After Macedonia had thus been reduced to complete political nullity and was left in possession of only as much power as was needful to guard the frontier of Hellas against the barbarians, steps were taken to dispose of the possessions ceded by the king. The Romans, who just at that time were learning by experience in Spain that transmarine provinces were a very dubious gain, and who had by no means begun the war with a view to the acquisition of territory, took none of the spoil for themselves, and thus compelled their allies also to moderation. They resolved to declare all the states of Greece, which had previously been under Philip, free; and Flamininus was commissioned to read the decree to that effect to the Greeks assembled at the Isthmian games (196). Thoughtful men doubtless might ask whether freedom was a blessing capable of being thus bestowed, and what was the value of freedom to a nation apart from union and unity; but the rejoicing was great and sincere, as the intention of the senate was sincere in conferring the freedom. . . .

In the rest of Greece Flamininus contented himself with exerting his influence, so far as he could do so without violence, over the internal affairs especially of the newly-freed communities; with placing the council and the courts in the hands of the more wealthy and bringing the anti-Macedonian party to the helm; and with attaching as much as possible the civic commonwealths to the Roman interest, by adding everything, which in each community should have fallen by martial law to the Romans, to the common property of the city concerned. The work was finished in the spring of 194; Flamininus once more assembled the deputies of all the Greek communities at Corinth, exhorted them to a rational and moderate use of the freedom conferred on them, and requested as the only return for the kindness of the Romans, that they would within thirty days send to him the Italian captives who had been sold into Greece during the Hannibalic war. Then he evacuated the last fortresses in which Roman garrisons were still stationed, Demetrias, Chalcis along with the smaller forts dependent upon it in Euboea, and Acrocorinthus—thus practically giving the lie to the assertion of the Aetolians that Rome had inherited from Philip the "fetters" of Greece—and departed homeward with all the Roman troops and the liberated captives.

It is only contemptible disingenuousness or weakly sentimentality, which can fail to perceive that the Romans were entirely in earnest with the liberation of Greece; and the reason why the plan so nobly projected resulted in so sorry a structure, is to be sought only in the complete moral and political disorganization of the Hellenic nation. It was no small matter, that a mighty nation should have suddenly with its powerful arm brought the land, which it had been accustomed to regard as its primitive home and as the shrine of its intellectual and higher interests, into the possession of full freedom, and should have conferred on every community in it deliverance from foreign taxation and foreign garrisons and the unlimited right of self-government; it is mere paltriness that sees in this nothing save political calculation. Political calculation made the liberation of Greece a possibility for the Romans; it was converted into a reality by the Hellenic sympathies that were at that time indescribably powerful in Rome, and above all in Flamininus himself. If the Romans are liable to any reproach, it is that all of them, in particular Flamininus who overcame the well-founded scruples of the senate, were hindered by the magic charm of the Hellenic name from perceiving in all its extent the wretched character of the Greek states of that period, and so allowed yet further freedom for the doings of communities which, owing to the impotent antipathies that prevailed alike in their internal and their mutual relations, knew neither how to act nor how to keep quiet. As things stood, it was really necessary at once to put an end to such a freedom, equally pitiful and pernicious, by means of a superior power permanently present on the spot; the feeble policy of sentiment, with all its apparent humanity, was far more cruel than the sternest occupation would have been. In Boeotia for instance Rome had, if not to instigate, at least to permit, a political murder, because the Romans had resolved to withdraw their troops from Greece and, consequently, could not prevent the Greeks friendly to Rome from seeking their remedy in the usual manner of the country. But Rome herself also suffered from the effects of this indecision. The war with Antiochus would not have arisen but for the political blunder of liberating Greece, and it would not have been dangerous but for the military blunder of withdrawing the garrisons from the principal fortresses on the European frontier. History has a Nemesis for every sin—for an impotent craving after freedom, as well as for an injudicious generosity.

Probably no modern scholar has done more to shape our understanding of Rome's initial contacts and early relations with the Greek world than MAURICE HOLLEAUX (1861–1932), professor at the Collège de France. Holleaux's influential volume, *Rome, la Grèce et les monarchies hellenistiques,* argues that Rome's knowledge of or contact with the east was very limited until the end of the third century. In this selection, therefore, he explains Rome's intervention in Greece as a sudden reversal of all previous policy. Holleaux throws out Mommsen's notion of philhellenism as a motivating element and stresses Roman calculation based on self-defense and irrational fear of Macedon and Syria.*

Maurice Holleaux

Preventive Warfare

It was probably late in the winter of 203–2 that Antiochus and Philip, apparently reviving the time-honoured coalition of Syria and Macedonia against Egypt, concluded the disgraceful agreement which roused Polybius' honest indignation—in fact, a lying compact which neither intended to keep. Then, in the spring, they got to work, without any pretence of justifying their aggressions. Antiochus invaded Southern Syria, but his operations are unknown and he seems to have achieved little. Philip, careless of the provisions of the partition treaty, sought to subdue, not towns subject to Egypt, but free cities; he wished to establish himself both on the Straits from the Hellespont to the Bosporus and in Caria, where he coveted Iasus, an excellent naval base.

He brought against Iasus Olympichus, probably a Carian dynast, his ally, who began to harry it. He himself directed operations on the Straits. There Lysimacheia, formerly Egyptian, in the Chersonese; Chalcedon, on the Bosporus; Cius, on the Propontis, were—since some unknown date—dependent allies of the Aetolian League. Philip imposed his alliance, *i.e.* his authority, upon Lysimacheia, expelled its Aetolian governor, and garrisoned it; he also occupied Chalcedon, and Perinthus, a Byzantine dependency lying between the two; then, acting as ally of Prusias, who had a quarrel with Cius, he besieged and took that town, but, before handing it over, sacked it and sold the population. Its neighbour Myrleia suffered the same fate. Returning to Macedonia,

*From Maurice Holleaux in *The Cambridge Ancient History* edited by S. A. Cook, F. E. Adcock, and M. P. Charlesworth (London: Cambridge University Press, 1954), vol. VIII, pp. 151–152, 155–160, 180–183, 237–240. Footnotes omitted.

Philip seized Thasos by treachery, so it is said, and, perhaps for some reason unknown to us, enslaved part of its inhabitants. It is noteworthy that he respected the Egyptian dependencies on the coast of Thrace.

This attack launched against inoffensive communities in profound peace raised a storm of indignation: the Greek world was outraged by the fate of Cius and Thasos. It also, beyond doubt, annoyed Antiochus, who was irritated by his ally's cool high-handedness, his co-operation with Prusias, a natural opponent of the Seleucids, and above all his occupation of Lysimacheia to which he himself had claims. Moreover, Philip's expedition naturally embroiled him with Aetolia, already angered by his non-observance of the treaty of 206, and Byzantium, and, more serious still, it made the Rhodians his declared enemies. His indirect attack upon Iasus, their friend, had moved them to protest, and they believed that his establishment upon the Straits endangered their trade; Philip added the last straw by making mock of them, promising, at their intercession, to spare Cius and then sacking it beneath the eyes of their envoys. Exasperated, and incited to action by an energetic citizen, Theophiliscus, whom they elected *navarch,* the Rhodians, peace-loving though they were, decided to fight Philip, bringing in also their allies, Byzantium, Cyzicus, Chios, Cos and the rest (end of summer 202).

Philip was unwise enough to despise Rhodes, but he feared the Romans, whose victory at Zama, during his maritime campaign, had freed them to intervene in the East. His spies at Rome kept him informed of their intentions; he soon had proof that these were not alarming. The Aetolians, furious but not daring to challenge him unaided, had attempted to renew friendly relations with the Senate and interest it in their cause (probably autumn 202 B.C.); but, harshly reminding their envoys of their "defection" in 206, the *patres* rejected their appeal. This rebuff implied that Rome had, at the moment, no mind to take action again in Greece against Macedonia; so Philip thought that he could safely pursue his eastern enterprises. He was, however, to meet adversaries whom he had rashly underrated. . . .

It was the obvious interest of Philip's enemies to raise up adversaries to him in the West. Attalus, who had remained the ally of the Aetolians after 206, had tried to move them, but in vain; their bad reception by the Senate had daunted them. He also thought not unnaturally of appealing to the Romans. It is true that, formally, he was neither their ally nor perhaps even their "friend" (*amicus populi Romani*), but they had included him in the peace of Phoenice and his relations with them were extremely cordial. On the other hand, the Rhodians, as we have seen, had been constantly opposed to Rome and were largely responsible for the defection of the Aetolians. But their fear of Philip led them to reverse their policy; it had made them ally themselves with Attalus, and now it decided them to appeal, like him, to Rome for help. In the late summer of 201 Pergamene and Rhodian envoys appeared before the Senate.

Careful of their dignity, the *patres* deferred giving any promise, but their decision was taken at once. About November Sulpicius Galba was re-elected consul; this meant that he would be commander in a new Macedonian war. "Macedonia" was indeed one of the consular provinces and fell to him.

This decision of the Senate, on the morrow of the struggle against Carthage, with people and army war-weary and longing for peace, the treasury empty, the

state-creditors restive, is most astonishing—the more so since Rome had certainly no grievance against Philip. The
force he is said to have sent to Hannibal
before Zama, and his aggressions against
certain unnamed "Greek allies of Rome"
are merely clumsy fabrications of later
times, invented to justify the hostile behaviour of the Roman government. In reality, fearing Rome greatly, Philip kept
peace with her most correctly. As for his
conflict with Attalus and Rhodes, that obviously could not justify the armed intervention of the Romans. Rhodes had naturally no title to their assistance; Attalus,
included in the recent peace, might claim
it in principle, but, in fact, he—like the
Rhodians—in attacking Philip had been
the aggressor. This war, decided upon so
quickly, was thus without legitimate cause;
it was simply willed by the Senate. A year
earlier, they had apparently no thought of
it: otherwise they would have forgotten for
the moment their grievances against Aetolia (as later in 200), and would have listened to her complaints against Philip.
Thus their conversion to a warlike policy
was sudden indeed.

The reason for this change—evidently a
strong one—is not directly known, for the
explanations given by our sources are quite
untrustworthy; it can only be inferred from
an examination of the circumstances. The
present writer would therefore indicate
what seems to him the most probable.

Attalus, a warm friend of Rome, the
Rhodians, serious, sensible, trusted and
esteemed, inspired confidence in the Senate. Knowing little of eastern affairs, the
patres must have listened attentively to
their representatives; doubtless their arguments greatly influenced the Roman decision, and we can conjecture, with some
probability, what they were. Apparently
the envoys laid little stress on the grievances of Attalus and Rhodes against Phil-

ip, since these were unlikely to move the
Senate, which would care little about the
seizure by Philip of some Hellespontine or
Asiatic towns whose very name was unknown in Rome. Wishing to persuade them
to fight Philip immediately, they must
have reviewed the matter from the standpoint of Roman interests, showing how
dangerous inaction would be to Rome, and
how easy it was to act at once. Rhodes and
Attalus had got wind of the compact between Antiochus and Philip; they had good
reasons for doubting its stability, but their
envoys could use it to frighten the Senate.
According to them, Antiochus was a conqueror from whom anything might be
feared; his understanding with Philip constituted a certain danger for Rome. At the
moment, the two kings aspired to make
Egypt their prey, but, once strengthened
by its spoils, what might they not do?
Would not Philip, ever the enemy of
Rome, bring in Antiochus against her? She
must break this threatening alliance by
crushing the ally within reach. Antiochus
was just then occupied in Syria, Philip,
much weakened, blockaded in Caria—it
was a fine opportunity to invade Macedonia. If Philip succeeded in returning home,
his defeat would nevertheless be swiftly
achieved. Rome would have with her, besides the Pergamene and Rhodian fleets,
the Aetolians thirsting for vengeance, Amy-
nander who had recently quarrelled with
Philip, and, of course, the barbarian enemies of Macedonia. Moreover, Philip's
Greek allies now hated him; his crimes at
Cius and Thasos aroused their common
horror; all Greece, doubtless, would join
Rome.

The ambassadors could not fail to move
the senators by talking of Antiochus. Rome
had no relations with him, but his resound-
ing fame had long made them uneasy.
Laevinus and Sulpicius had many times in
Greece heard first the Aetolians, then At-

talus, relate his exploits; Laevinus was in Pergamum when Antiochus returned from the Far East; and the Alexandrians had recently asked for protection against him. The Romans were very ready to see an enemy in every monarch, and Antiochus, so powerful, fortunate, and undoubtedly of unbounded ambitions, seemed especially disquieting. They pictured him lord of the fabulous treasures, the unnumbered hosts of Asia; he reminded them at once of Xerxes and of Alexander; above all, he was for them the unknown that is terrible. When they heard that he was secretly in league with Philip, his hostility to them seemed beyond doubt. Conqueror of the East, he would assuredly dispute the West with Rome, thus helping Philip to his revenge.

Therefore it was necessary to take prompt measures to counteract this danger, profit by Antiochus' momentary absence to act against Philip—not to destroy him (a too difficult and lengthy undertaking), but cripple him and, further, drive him from Greece. Greece which had hitherto meant little to the Senate, since they did not fear Philip alone, suddenly assumed peculiar importance: it was the natural point of concentration for the two kings, their common base against Italy. They must, accordingly, be prevented from using it, and it must at the same time be brought under Roman control. Not that there was any question of subjugating it— that would have been to provide Philip and Antiochus with the profitable role of "liberator." This role Rome would assume herself; she would restore Greek freedom, destroyed or restricted by Philip, thereby securing the enthusiastic gratitude of the Greeks, and then constitute herself their permanent protectress. Liberated and shielded by Rome, Greece would be closed to the kings, Rome's enemies, closed to Antiochus if, after Philip's defeat, he should

pursue alone the aggressive designs concerted with him.

Such, it seems, were the fears and calculations which gave rise to the warlike policy of the Senate, hitherto so little inclined to entangle itself in Eastern affairs. Apparently aggressive, but really preventive, its object was to checkmate the dangerous purposes attributed to Antiochus and Philip, and, with this aim, make Greece the outwork of Italy's defences to the East. It is, however, quite possible that these leading motives were reinforced by subsidiary considerations of sentiment: the longing to cancel an inglorious peace and punish Philip for his alliance with Carthage, a proud desire in some Romans to conquer the unconquerable Macedonians, and also accomplish something spectacular in extending Roman primacy over the illustrious peoples of Greece. Of an over-romantic ardent sympathy for the Greeks, Philip's victims, such as is often attributed to the Senate, the present writer can find no clear evidence. The Roman nobility had steeped itself in Hellenic culture, but had no tenderness for Greeks, as the late war had shown plainly enough. Their philhellenism confined itself to things of the spirit, and was not allowed to be a factor in their public actions. They were, it is true, going to use against Philip a "philhellenic" policy, but only as Hannibal, for instance, had used a "philitalian" policy against Rome—because it suited their purpose, not through love of Greece.

However urgent may have been Attalus and the Rhodians, Rome could not begin the war before 200 B.C. The Senate had first to make ready for it. Military preparation was easy: Macedonia was known to be drained of men, and if Philip returned before the Romans arrived, he would only dispose of a very limited field-army, the more as he would have to garrison his many strongholds in Greece. It would be enough to pit against him a normal consular army of two legions, especially as Rome counted upon numerous allies; and this army would partly be raised by the enlistment, nominally voluntary, of veterans returning from Africa. As for the fleet, Pergamene and Rhodian assistance would allow of its reduction to some 50 warships. Under such conditions the war would cost little. However, as the treasury was depleted, the repayment of loans contracted during the Hannibalic War had to be suspended, and to disarm the opposition of creditors the Senate decided to indemnify them by large concessions of public land.

There remained the main achievement of statecraft, the political preparation for the war, that is the creation in peace time of a clash between Rome and Philip which would inevitably result in war. This seemed a difficult problem; for, as we have noticed, Rome had no grievance against Philip, and if the Senate desired war, it stood alone in desiring it. Philip would do anything to avoid war if he were allowed to negotiate, and would not shrink from even considerable concessions provided they were not dishonouring. As for the Roman people, upon whose vote everything ultimately depended, its feelings were entirely peaceful. In this apparently embarrassing situation the Senate, despite what has often been asserted, experienced no difficulty; supreme in matters of foreign policy and unhampered by scruples, it manoeuvred so that Philip and the Roman citizens were driven into a war which neither desired. It had only to present to Philip, without previous negotiation, an offensive ultimatum based on an imaginary casus belli, then use his refusal to comply with it to secure the people's vote for war.

According to the ius fetiale, Philip—although, in fact, he had committed no offence—must be confronted with a "demand for satisfaction" (rerum repetitio). This demand was drawn up by the Senate, who contrived to turn it into an intolerable provocation. It is summarized thus by Polybius: "Philip was to grant to Attalus, for injuries caused to him, reparations to be fixed by arbitrators; if he complied, he might consider himself at peace with Rome, but if he refused, the consequences would be the reverse." It can be seen how insulting was the form of this demand: without giving him any opportunity of justifying himself, Rome exacted from Philip, under threat of war, immediate submission. But the substance was even worse; in plain contradiction to the facts, Philip was represented as the aggressor; the Roman ultimatum really amounted to this: the Pergamene fleet, together with the Rhodian, had attacked the Macedonian fleet at Chios, therefore the successor of Alexander must humiliate himself before the parvenu kinglet of Pergamum.

But the Senate went still further: its rerum repetitio was preceded by the injunction that "Philip should make war henceforth upon no Greek state." This was outrageous from the standpoint of international law. In the first place, by what right did the Romans concern themselves with Greek interests? They had now no Greek allies. Secondly, in 204, they had recognized Philip's full sovereignty and implicitly admitted his authority over many Greeks. Now, without urging any reasons, they claimed, contrary to treaty, to reverse this state of affairs. In denying Philip the right to make war upon Greeks, they impaired his sovereignty, and virtually destroyed the authority which he exercised in Greece, for it became a mere illusion if he might not uphold it by force; and, finally, by implication they declared unjustified all former wars waged by himself or his predecessors against Greeks, and thus denied validity to results of their victories. The destruction of all that Macedon had achieved in Greece since Philip II was in fact what the Senate demanded. It demanded the impossible, but in this it showed its skill, for it drove Philip to extremes and also, by declaring the Greeks immune from attack, won them over (at least so it hoped) to the side of Rome, and stated a principle which it could, at need, apply later to Antiochus. . . .

It is clear that the Senate, though going beyond the terms of the preliminaries, yet treated Philip without excessive harshness. The war indemnity was bearable; he lost his navy (a precaution justified by his former Adriatic enterprises), but his military power, despite some annalists, suffered no limitation. Doubtless the *patres* considered it wise not to drive Philip to extremes, but their comparative moderation had, as soon appeared, another cause—they planned to use him, at need, against Antiochus.

Their decree contained, moreover, two provisions of capital importance. The first showed that Rome aimed at more than merely peace with Philip; it affected all the Greeks then independent and never subject to the king. By pronouncing that they were to remain "free and autonomous," she guaranteed their independence and forced Philip to do the same, thus constituting herself the permanent protectress of Hellenic freedom wherever it existed. This was the logical outcome of her whole policy and was already implied in her command to Philip, in 200, to abstain from hostilities against any Greek people; but—and this is significant—the Greeks of Asia, *i.e.* the inhabitants of the autonomous towns, were now expressly mentioned together with the Greeks of Europe: Antiochus was consequently barred from any enterprise against these towns. A second provision related to the cities and populations still subject to Philip. The fact that the Senate pronounced upon them all signified that all were by right of conquest at the exclusive disposal of Rome. This principle once formulated, a distinction was made between the cities in Greece proper and those outside it. Philip was to evacuate the latter, *i.e.* those in Asia, the Islands, and Thrace, expressly mentioned, and "leave them free": so Rome, after emphasizing her rights over them, granted them liberty forthwith—a liberty which, of course, all had to respect. Rome's eagerness to do this is easily explained: Philip's eastern possessions were directly threatened by Antiochus, who already occupied almost all those in Asia; Rome hastened to let him know that they were not to be touched and that his annexations consequently could not be recognized as legitimate. . . .

The Aetolians, naturally, asserted that "Greece was merely changing masters, the Romans replacing Philip, as the only result of the war." Flamininus was pained to find these statements widely repeated and believed; it was important to reassure the Greeks, to convince them, without delay, of Roman disinterestedness. They were reassured by the striking manifesto at the Isthmian Games—a *coup de théâtre* arranged by Flamininus to impress their imagination and provoke their applause.

At the Isthmian festival (June–July 196), before the opening of the Games, the herald, advancing into the stadium, proclaimed: "The Roman Senate and the consul Titus Quinctius, having overcome king Philip and the Macedonians, leave free, without garrisons or tribute, and governed by their ancestral laws, the Corinthians, Phocians, [Eastern] Locrians, Euboeans, Phthiotic Achaeans, Magnesians, Thessalians and Perrhaebians." This proclamation, which the herald had to repeat, evoked frenzied enthusiasm, the more ardent as the anxiety had been so intense.

The crowd nearly suffocated Flamininus in their outburst of joy. He had—for a time—his heart's desire: he was the idol of the Greeks, the Aetolians and probably the Boeotians alone excepted. In fact, in accordance with his promises, the Romans kept nothing in Greece; the Corinthian declaration splendidly completed what had been begun by the decree about the peace: in this decree Rome had guaranteed liberty to all Greeks who then enjoyed it and had restored it to Philip's former eastern subjects; she now restored liberty to his former subject-allies in Greece.

This was true. Yet the "liberated" Greeks in Corinth did not obtain complete *eleutheria*. Rome, reviving the time-honoured formula of Antigonus and renouncing the oppressive rights of victors, imposed upon them neither tribute, garrisons, nor foreign laws, but she retained authority over them. This appeared when, after the Isthmian Games, the Commissioners, presided over by Flamininus, proceeded to the "settlement of Hellenic affairs." They settled the political status of the freed peoples as absolutely as that of the Illyrians wrested from Philip, who were allotted generally to Pleuratus. . . .

According to a generally accepted opinion, the decisive struggle in which Rome engaged, first against Macedonia, then against Syria, was, in essence, not indeed a struggle for territorial aggrandizement, but a struggle for wealth and even more for power, initiated by the imperialistic ambition of the Senate. . . .

The Romans were certainly not indifferent to money (as is proved by the example of Manlius and Fulvius) or to power: their victory over Antiochus, the thought that they had no longer a rival, filled them with pride. Yet it does not follow nor does it seem probable to the present writer that it was greed of wealth and

empire which determined their course of action. Indeed it is most noteworthy that they never thought of turning their victories to economic advantage: the treaties which they made contained no commercial stipulation in their own favour (though the treaty of Apamea contained one in favour of Rhodes), and they did not impose tribute on any of the peoples whom they conquered—a sufficiently clear proof that in deciding on their policy they were little if at all obsessed by thoughts of gain. And, as we have seen, not one of their political acts from 200 to 188 bears the clear stamp of imperialism or cannot be explained except by a passion for domination. The attribution to the Senate of "Eastern plans" or of a "Mediterranean programme" which it was only waiting for a favourable opportunity to carry out, is no more than arbitrary conjecture, unsupported by the facts. There is nothing to show that in 200 the *patres* were more attracted than before to Greek lands or that their eastern policy, hitherto entirely dictated by the needs of the moment, changed its character at that date. Everything leads us to believe that then, as before, their intervention was merely the result of external circumstances which seemed to impose action upon them. As in 229 they would not have crossed the Adriatic but for the provocation offered them by Teuta, and in 214 would not have gone into Greece but for the necessity of countering the alliance of Philip with Hannibal, so, in all likelihood, they would not have turned eastward again but for their discovery of the alliance between Philip and Antiochus and the threat which they saw in it.

The truth is that they imagined themselves to be threatened when they were not. The insincere alliance of the two kings was in no way aimed at them; and, moreover, when they did allow it to alarm them, it was already breaking down. If their intervention had been less prompt, they would probably have seen the erstwhile allies open enemies: a war would have broken out between them, which would have freed Rome from all anxiety from that quarter. In any event, as is shown by his prompt seizure of Lysimacheia, Philip would have prevented Antiochus from setting foot in Europe, and so would have vanished even the phantom of that "Seleucid peril" which, from the first, was the constant preoccupation of the Romans. Indeed it was their act, when they crippled Philip thinking thereby to weaken Antiochus, that allowed the latter a free road westwards and enabled him to cross the Hellespont. But, even then, there was, as we have seen, no real Seleucid peril. If it ever existed, it was in 192, when the Great King marched down into Greece with Hannibal in his train, and it was again the Romans who created it by their errors of policy, the fruit of their vain alarms. To guard against an imaginary threat of aggression they were unconscionably persistent in urging Antiochus to withdraw from Europe and their offensive insistence only succeeded in exhausting his patience. By an ironic paradox, the two enterprises which brought them so much glory and laid the foundation of their world-supremacy had their origin in a groundless fear. Had they been more keen-sighted and less easily alarmed, they would not have come to dominate the Hellenic world. More probably they would have concentrated their efforts in the neighbouring barbarian countries west of Italy—and that with more reason and more advantage to themselves.

If they were thus misled by unfounded fears it was due partly to the suspicious temper of the Senate which inclined them to detect only too readily dangerous neighbours plotting the ruin of Rome, partly to their profound ignorance of eastern affairs. The *patres* had omitted to inform themselves about these matters, and strangely neglected for a long time to do so— one is surprised to find, for example, that in 196 they had not got wind of the treaty about to be concluded between Antiochus and Egypt. Lacking the knowledge necessary for forming an opinion of their own, they believed what they were told and were curiously swayed by foreign influences. This was no new thing: it has been maintained, and with much probability, that the quarrel between Rome and Carthage over Spain was largely due to the reports and intrigues of the Massiliotes in Rome. It is even more certain that the real authors of the Second Macedonian War were Attalus and Rhodes, and that the war against Antiochus was mainly the work of Eumenes—the same Eumenes who was to have so large a hand in bringing about the war against Perseus. So far as the East is concerned, the Senate, so jealous of its authority and reputed so clear-sighted, only saw through the eyes of others and only acted upon the impulse of others—of others who had an interest in impelling it to act. After 200 B.C. in their eastern policy the Romans, little as they knew it, followed where he led: while they thought they were only providing for the safety of Rome, they were, in reality, serving the cause and furthering the interests of Pergamum and Rhodes.

Judgments of praise or blame on the nature of Roman imperialism may be irrelevant. Perhaps the attitudes and principles under which Rome operated in expanding her control overseas grew naturally out of the system developed at home. This is the thesis brilliantly expounded by E. BADIAN (b. 1925) in his *Foreign Clientelae*, probably the most important work on the subject of Roman expansion produced in the last two decades. Trained in New Zealand, Oxford, and Rome, Badian is presently professor of classics and history at the State University of New York at Buffalo. In this work, he analyzes Roman attitudes toward Greek states as an outgrowth and application of the diplomatic policies pursued toward Italian states and toward Carthage.*

E. Badian

A Logical Development

Little is known of Roman relations with Greece and the East before the First Illyrian War. There are stories of early contacts; but whatever truth there may be in them, there was no permanent friendship or close association. We have seen how the Pyrrhic War first made Eastern nations interested in the Western barbarians; but there is no sign of more than passing curiosity. Holleaux has demolished—once and for all, one hopes—the extravagant theories, once fashionable, of Roman interventions in Eastern politics and Roman treaties of "friendship" or "alliance" with Greek monarchs and republics. Little remains of these conjectures but a state of "friendship" with Egypt and perhaps with some other countries; a state not taken very seriously by anyone and amounting to no more than mutual awareness. It was not out of relations like these that Roman intervention in the East finally developed.

It arose directly out of the protectorate Rome had now assumed over Italy and her usual fear of dangerous neighbours. The States of Italy were by now firmly united under her hegemony and in practice could not defend their own interests just as the Latins had once depended on Rome for protection against the hill-tribes the whole of Italy now depended on her for protection against aggressors from outside. Yet Rome, as her own security increased, was already less willing to meet her moral obligations. Thus, though many complaints had been made about interfer-

*From E. Badian, *Foreign Clientelae, 264-70 B.C.* (Oxford: The Clarendon Press, 1967), pp. 43-45, 62-75, 82-83. Reprinted by permission of The Clarendon Press, Oxford. Footnotes omitted.

ence by Illyrian pirates with Italian trade, the Senate had turned a deaf ear to them. It was only when a major power seemed to be developing east of the Adriatic that it decided to take action. We have seen how Rome commonly used the protection of weaker states as a means of furthering her own policy. It was in this way that she used the complaints of the Italians as soon as she deemed her interests to be involved east of the Adriatic, and began a preventive war against the Illyrian kingdom under Teuta.

I have tried elsewhere to discuss in detail the causes and the effects of the First Illyrian War, that turning-point in Roman history to which modern historians have in general paid so little attention. It marks the first extension of Roman influence east of the Adriatic; and—what is no less important—the further development of the principle of association without treaty, the genesis of which we have noticed in Sicily. After a rapid campaign, a chain of states dependent on Rome in this elusive way was established in Illyria: the cities of Corcyra, Apollonia, Dyrrhachium (Epidamnus) and Issa, and probably the tribes of the Parthini and Atintanes, became informal friends of Rome; another "friend," Demetrius of Pharus, was made (or soon became) *de facto* ruler of the Illyrian kingdom. . . .

We now come to the outbreak of the Second Macedonian War; and the events that led up to it are surpassed in obscurity only by its causes. The former—fortunately—do not concern us as such; at the latter we must glance before proceeding.

We have seen that the Peace of Phoenice did not, as Holleaux thought, mark the end of Roman interest in Greece and the East. He has, indeed, only one main argument in support of his view: the treatment of the Aetolian embassy that came to ask for Roman support, probably in 202. But, even if this embassy is historical—which is far from certain—, we know nothing about its outcome except that Rome did not help the Aetolians, probably on the grounds that the alliance no longer existed. This, however, is not surprising, especially considering that Roman attention must have been concentrated on North Africa, where (before Zama) the war was not by any means decided. To involve herself, at this critical time, in a war with Philip, by the side of allies who (apart from all else) had already shown themselves unable to stand up to him, would be inexcusable folly and might well endanger the situation in Illyria which Rome was so carefully maintaining; for the Hannibalic War had strained Italian manpower to the utmost and, until the war was finished, there was no certainty that the strain would not again increase. The historian knows that there was no danger: the Senate knew only the past.

Roman interest in the East was limited to securing Illyria and merely watching Greece. The Senate had wanted peace with Philip. But now Philip had shown that peace with him was dangerous: if he were allowed to continue his activities, the whole of Illyria might change its allegiance. This was the state of affairs when Rhodes and Attalus sent envoys in 201, reporting Philip's aggression in the East and his "pact" with Antiochus. Action was quick and bellicose. Galba, a "Macedonian expert," was elected consul, and in the spring of next year a Roman embassy crossed to Greece and visited Philip's most important Greek allies, proclaiming the new Roman policy, a statement of which they finally handed to the King's general, Nicanor. They met Attalus at Athens and seem to have given him some assurances; but they had to be careful, especially as the Roman Assembly had not yet voted for war. They then stayed in Rhodes, where they were informed that this vote had at last been passed; thereupon they sent Lepidus (one of their members) to deliver the formal declaration of war to Philip, and proceeded to Syria and Egypt—for what purpose and with what results is uncertain, but certainly in connexion with the war about to begin. This quick decision to attack Philip need not surprise us as much as it surprises those who attribute to the Fathers a complete lack of interest in the East between 205 and 201. But it is, in any case, a change and needs explaining. No one line of explanation, though, is enough. Holleaux attributes it to fear of the pact between Philip and Antiochus, which the Rhodian and Pergamene envoys announced in Rome; Rome, he thinks, tended to believe that all kings were the natural enemies of the Republic. Though there is little evidence for such a belief— only of anti-Roman propaganda attributing it to Rome—and it is indeed absurd to imagine anything of the sort at a time when Rome was about to wage war in defence of Attalus, it is no doubt true that rumour of the pact with the remote and famed Antiochus must have made Philip seem a potential threat. But we must not overstress this: for Philip had not fared too well in his Eastern campaign, and there had been little trace of any help for him from the Seleucid. Attalus and Rhodes knew this, and the Romans must have heard of it before their army crossed the Adriatic. Yet they decided to prosecute the war. Nor did they at any time fear an invasion of Italy: for no preparations (such as we shall later meet before the war with Antiochus) were made to counter such a threat. Griffith, recognizing the insufficiency of this motive, has added to it Roman fear of Philip's renewed naval power. This can hardly have been very important: in 201 Rome had no interests in the

Aegean, and a fleet operating there was not the sort of thing to frighten the Senate into war—especially as that fleet had shown its inability to master those of Rhodes and Pergamum, and as it had, in any case, contained only fifty-three cataphracts even before the battle of Chios and ceased to be a danger after it.

These and other reasons may in varying degrees have influenced the Senate—but none of them seems sufficient to justify a major war at a time when Roman manpower and economic resources needed nothing more than recovery. And we are driven to recognizing that the Illyrian situation contains a main part of the answer to our question: the Senate had tried a policy of peace with Philip and failed, and now war seemed inevitable. Besides, more irrational motives must (as so often) have played an important part. Philip had tried to stab Rome in the back when she was, he thought, on the point of defeat by Hannibal. And the Romans did not forgive their enemies, especially those whom they thought treacherous. We shall see, in the case of the Third Punic War, how the spirit of stark hatred could intervene in Roman politics, even against political interest. In the same way, we may well believe, many senators in 201 may have felt that the time for their revenge had come: Philip was in trouble in the East and had made powerful enemies; Rome had defeated her only great antagonist—it was time to pay the King back in his own coin. Who were the propounders of this policy, we cannot tell with certainty. It has been suggested that Scipio was opposed to it. But there is no evidence for this, and indeed it is not certain that he, with experience only of war and diplomacy in the West, had any set Eastern policy on his return. Galba and Tuditanus, the principal Eastern experts, supported it: Galba was made consul and sent to Greece;

Tuditanus was on the mission which presented the ultimatum and visited Syria and Egypt. Cotta, the other consul, was related to M. Cotta, whom we found in Illyria: the aggressive policy, it seems, had the support of the "Eastern lobby." It was these men, no doubt, who knew Philip's weakness and who had discovered how the Greeks could be turned against him, especially at a time when his treachery and cruelty had already made a strong impression upon them. It was they, moreover, who knew that Illyria would only be safe when Macedon had been humbled.

The method chosen to achieve this appears in the ultimatum which the Roman mission proclaimed to the principal leagues of Greece and finally handed to Nicanor. Philip was not to wage war on any Greeks and was to submit his dispute with Attalus to arbitration; only on these conditions could he live in peace with Rome. The subtlety of these conditions is greater than has sometimes been seen: for some historians have thought them brutal demands, running counter to all justice to such an extent as to ensure rejection and war. But it is clear that Rome did not want war, if the same result could be achieved peacefully: it was perhaps unlikely that the terms would be accepted— for Rome had no legal *locus standi*, and Philip would see their long-range implications; but if they were, so much the better. The caution of the Roman embassy at Athens is not due *entirely* to the fact that they "had to drive two unwilling parties into conflict, the Roman people and Philip": it may have been partly due to hopes of a peace with honour and advantage. For the real aim, as is seen in the peace made after the war, was to make Philip into a client prince and (as an inevitable consequence) Greece into a protectorate.

There is nothing harsh in the request that Philip's differences with Attalus

should be discussed before an imperial tribunal: Holleaux, and those who follow him, must not be allowed to usurp the function of the court that never sat and— without evidence—persuade us of Philip's innocence. Much—even the respective chronology of the battles of Lade and Chios—has been made to hinge on this assertion; yet, on investigation, we must suspend judgement. For all we know is that Attalus' fleet was present at Chios, but not at Lade; that Philip invaded Pergamene territory; and that Theophiliscus of Rhodes persuaded Attalus to take strong action. We do not know the order of these events, and we do not know what action is referred to. We have only Philip's word against the Senate's (i.e. that of Attalus' envoys). And in any case, it is more than likely that Rhodes and Attalus could make out a *prima facie* case. The Senate's proposal, whatever the true facts, was not "in plain contradiction" to what facts it was likely to know. Nor does the other demand go as far as has been suggested; for it only means that Philip should cease attacking Greek states. It is wildly extravagant to claim that this simple demand "by implication ... declared unjustified all former wars waged by himself or his predecessors against Greeks, and thus denied validity to the result of their victories." It might as easily be claimed that present-day demands that certain powers should stop their policy of aggression seek to confine the powers concerned to their frontiers of several hundred years ago. In fact there is not even the more moderate claim of the "freedom of the Hellenes": Rome had not yet moved quite as far as that.

In fact the Roman ultimatum is only a further extension of an old Roman political idea, which we have seen at work quite often: just as, originally, Rome had invented a method of evading the requirements of fetial law—that wars must be waged only in defence of one's own or of allied territory—by making alliances with, and thereby assuming "legitimate" protection over, states actually facing attack, so now states were unilaterally taken under Roman protection without even the formality of a treaty. This is a natural consequence of the greater elasticity that Roman diplomatic categories had acquired since 264, though its practical effect was, of course, to do away with the last restrictions (except purely formal ones) which fetial law imposed upon policy. In the two generations since Roman armies first crossed the sea, the system of the Confederacy, already made less rigid by the ambiguous status of the Latins after 338, had—as we have seen—been practically abandoned as far as further expansion was concerned. Instead, there had grown up a system of informal connexion with free states, beginning in Sicily and further tested in Illyria, the elastic obligations of which fitted into the Roman habits of social thought which we know as "clientela" and, while thus acquiring moral sanction, also fitted in well with the practical requirements of power politics. As this system was extended and became firmly established, it even transformed by its influence the earlier concept of *amicitia*—which Rome knew well, e.g. in the case of Massilia or Egypt—until the Romans could no longer imagine the co-existence of genuinely equal states: her *amici* could only be her clients.

But this was still in the future. In the meantime, Rome presented her ultimatum on behalf of her new friends, the Greeks. If Philip rejected it—as was likely—, it meant war; and Rome was prepared and had a fair cause and good allies. If he accepted it—and, as we have seen, it was not so intolerably harsh as to preclude this— and withdrew from his new conquests, he would cease to be a danger and become dependent on Rome, though to all appearances still a powerful monarch. For his schemes of expansion in the East would have gone the way of those in the West; and to the Greeks he would be the humbled aggressor and Rome the champion—a reversal of roles which his influence even among his old Greek allies could not long survive. However, despite all this it might have been better for him to accept humiliation and wait for his chance— Rome's clash with Antiochus, and the reversal of Greek feeling, both of which he might have promoted. But he was outraged by Roman arrogance and faithlessness and decided on war.

The war thus arose from a complex of causes: principally Roman fear and Roman hatred, but also Philip's decision not to submit. Rome, though she had no legal justification for it, created a pretext by an extension of traditional practice—an extension which, though legally perhaps unwarranted, is historically quite comprehensible in the light of the development of Roman diplomatic categories since 264. And this, in the course of war, led to that important event, the "liberation" of the Greeks.

. . . Considering the paucity of reliable sources, we are fortunate in being able to trace fairly clearly the origins and development of the idea of "the freedom of Greece." At first, as we have seen, Roman ideas did not go beyond the "protection" of Philip's recent victims: in 200 he is asked only to stop waging war on Greeks— the fact, and the manner of it, had turned Greek sentiment against him, and the request was bound to be popular. There is no thought of freeing (say) the Thessalians or the Corinthians, or even—except by diplomatic means—of detaching the Achaean League: when Lepidus, in the interview before Abydus, mentions the victims Rome is protecting, they are only those of Philip's recent campaigns. Philip remembered this, and when he saw his hopes fading, tried to make peace more or less on these terms: he offered to give up all he had ever conquered and asked if that was enough. But by then (198) it was not. For Flamininus, with whom he then negotiated, was the bearer of the Senate's new policy. This new policy demanded (apart from reparations) the evacuation of the whole of Greece. When Philip, at the conference on the Aous, asked what cities he was required to liberate, Flamininus began with the Thessalians. And at the conference at Nicaea, though Flamininus here may have played a double game, it is clear that Philip had no real chance of peace on any other terms: the first question the Senate later asked his envoys in Rome was whether he was willing to give up the "fetters of Greece."

Precisely how the new policy arose, between 200 and 198, we cannot tell. It is not likely to have been Flamininus' own invention: a young man of no position, he must have had powerful backing to gain his command. But he was, as it turned out, the right man for the situation, and the comparative failure of his predecessors—for when Flamininus took over, Philip still held the Aous gorge, and Rome's allies had been severely defeated and had lost interest in the war—must have made it clear to many senators that a new approach was advisable. That is probably why a talented and ambitious young man was sent out and given good veteran reinforcements and a good propagandist policy. The effect was immediate. The Aous conference served as the stage for the dramatic announcement of the policy (Flamininus was an adept at *coups de théâtre*), and the battle of the Gorge was Philip's first serious defeat. And by November of that year we find the greater part of Greece fighting by the side of the consul: in particular, the Achaean League had been won

over. But the new policy was not only propaganda, designed to impress the Greeks: it represented solid Roman interests. For it had become clear to the Senate that the demand that Philip should give up his conquests was strategically as well as politically insufficient. The Greek allies demanded Philip's complete withdrawal from Greece, and in particular from the three "fetters of Greece": unless Demetrias, Chalcis and Acrocorinth were given up, they could not feel secure—and thus Rome learnt that, unless she too insisted on this condition, the war might turn out to have been fought in vain. It is thus likely that the new policy arose out of the lessons learnt in the course of the war. In any case, the demand that Philip should evacuate Greece was formulated by Flamininus and the Greek allies into a common platform.

But this platform was not yet the "freedom of the Greeks": it is given by Polybius, more modestly, as withdrawal from the whole of Greece. This, then, is the stage Roman plans had reached by 198: in 200, Philip was to stop attacking the Greeks; now he was to withdraw from the whole of Greece. But there was still no mention of what was to happen to Greece after his withdrawal. For at the time one had to take care not to offend the allies, who were all hoping for some of the spoils: even if the Senate's mind was made up—and nothing suggests that it was: the Senate was not given to facing problems of organization before they arose—the new policy could have propaganda value only in its negative form.

It is only after the war has been won at Cynoscephalae that we at last come to the "freedom of the Greeks." And again, the implications are not yet those of the Isthmian declaration. By now the question of organizing the territory Philip was to give up had to be faced, especially as Antiochus was approaching Europe with an army. And now for the first time Flamininus informed the Aetolians that cities which had surrendered to the *fides* of Rome would not be given up to them. The Aetolians were enraged at what they considered deceit; but the rest of the Greeks approved: for it was now clear to them that the "liberated" Greek cities could expect not to be handed over to new masters. The attitude of the Romans themselves to their conquests, however, remained in doubt even after the Senate's commissioners arrived bearing its decree. It began: "All the Greeks not under Philip's rule in both Asia and Europe are to be free and live according to their own laws," and went on to stipulate that those under Philip's rule were to be handed over to the Romans before the Isthmian Games, except for (in practice) those too far distant to be occupied by the Romans; these were to be free. It was obvious that the Romans would permit no other masters in Greece, European and Asiatic—the warning to Antiochus was plain, and it was underlined by the request to Prusias to free Cius. But it was not by any means obvious what the Romans were going to do with the cities over which they could claim rights of conquest from Philip. The Asiatic ones were declared "free"— this was convenient for Rome, and indeed no good alternative was possible. But were they going to occupy those in Europe? The Aetolians, despite Polybius' prejudiced account, had good reason to fear it. For, as we hear, the Senate itself had not made up its mind about the "fetters of Greece": the Greeks were now within an ace of reaping the harvest of their excessive insistence on the importance of these places. Only after a good deal of discussion did Flamininus convince the ten commissioners that for Rome they were not worth retaining: the goodwill of the Greeks (especially the Achaeans) would be a greater asset, particu-

larly as the Aetolians were offended beyond remedy. But this decision, in the meantime, was kept secret, while Flamininus staged his greatest *coup de théâtre*—it was only the proclamation at the Isthmian games that assured the Greeks that (in theory, at least) they were all to be free, and that the Romans would not assume any of the burdens and privileges of sovereignty.

Much has been written about the proclamation and what it implied. Subtle webs have been spun about the difference between the Greeks declared free directly by the *Senatus consultum* and those freed by the proclamation; and Polybius, who knows no such difference, has been accused of misunderstanding it. It has been said that the declaration of freedom was drawn from the Hellenistic political arsenal, and even that Rome cunningly adapted it to her purpose. It cannot be denied that by 197/6 the Senate *may* have been influenced by the history of Polyperchon and Antigonus: Flamininus would certainly have known it. But I hope to have shown that the "freedom of the Greeks" is not, as is sometimes thought, a new idea in Roman diplomacy, for which foreign origins have to be posited, but a natural development of Roman policy, due to strategic political experience. The idea itself is thoroughly Roman: if we subtract the pomp and grandiloquence—which alone we may safely ascribe to Flamininus' knowledge of Greek history and ideas, as much as to his character—the declaration that the Greeks were to be free does not differ from the (less spectacular) earlier decisions that Segesta or the Illyrian coast were to be free: it was a declaration of *nolle episcopari*. Nor is there any real difference between the Greeks "originally free" and those once "under Philip's rule." Both groups were in the same class: free *amici* of Rome. The differences noticed by Täubler were as unknown to the Senate as to Polybius: for it sent its commissioners to "establish firmly the freedom of the Greeks"—without distinction. Thus the idea is Roman, and (as this whole account has tried to show) its application is the result of four years of fighting and diplomacy, during which we can see Roman policy gradually leading up to it. Nor was there any cunning adaptation: when the Senate declares the Greeks "free," it really means them to be legally free—except in so far as gratitude would oblige them to respect Rome's will. The limitation turned out to be severe; but it was extra-legal. And it was the only limitation. Also, such as it was, it applied to *all* the Greeks: for they all had their freedom by a *munus populi Romani.* The legal theory of those who maintain that a "unilateral" declaration of freedom was necessarily precarious, because it could be "unilaterally" withdrawn, is fundamentally vicious: the freedom of (say) the Thessalians could not be withdrawn by the Senate any more than that of New Zealand or India can be withdrawn by the British Parliament, which "unilaterally" granted it. As we have seen, even the freed slave did not hold his freedom precariously. Where the Senate meant a benefit to be precarious, this had to be unequivocally stated. And no one ever mentions such a provision even in the cases—e.g. those of the Sicilian cities after the *lex Rupilia*—where freedom is at its lowest and our information at its best.

How Rome regarded her position with respect to her Greek friends became clear immediately. Flamininus and the commissioners went about adapting constitutions, arranging leagues, and being generally helpful. In Boeotia Flamininus even became involved in party intrigues to the extent of (perhaps unwittingly) lending help in a political assassination. This instance, discreditable as it is, provides the best proof of the fact that Rome did not regard herself as sovereign and the Greeks as subjects: for if Flamininus had been able to make direct demands, the whole unsavoury business would have been unnecessary. Later again, when war is declared against Nabis, to complete the work of liberation, no one thinks of ordering the Greeks to join in it: Flamininus expounds the situation and politely asks for their decision—which can, of course, be taken for granted. After the war, Roman troops are withdrawn from the fetters of Greece, and with a paternal speech Rome leaves the Greeks to their freedom. . . .

There is no change in Roman motives—only a shift of emphasis in Roman methods. The "freedom of Greece" was a piece of (by that time) traditional Roman diplomacy. Rome had (partly by accident) discovered the value of the "free" friend, especially in the cases of Saguntum and the Illyrians: he acted as a centre for gathering information and also as an outpost and a shock-absorber; if he was attacked, Rome was in the pleasant position of being able to decide whether and when to assist him—Saguntum had not been helped till it was too late and the Illyrians not at all (except by means of an envoy), and little attention had been paid to the Illyrian kings at Phoenice. Thus this policy of solid advantages combined with elastic liabilities was now applied to the Greeks, with a propagandist twist to suit their traditions. It was soon found (if it had not, indeed, always been known) that it could not be extended to Asia; and so the Romans, demanding a concession from Antiochus in return for their not occupying European Greece, fell back on another diplomatic category they knew well: the demarcation line. This again is often described as a Hellenistic and un-Roman concept; yet Rome had been practising it for centuries: ever since the first treaty with Carthage the demarcation line—against Tarentum, against Pyrrhus (who was requested to leave Italy), against Hasdrubal—had been a stock device of Roman diplomacy. Now the Senate demanded that, as Hasdrubal had once undertaken to remain beyond the Ebro, so Antiochus should undertake to remain beyond the Hellespont. This would have given Rome security. The Hellespont, like the Ebro, was a perfect "natural" demarcation line—not in the sense that it was easy to defend, but in that any violation would be patent and undeniable. An arbitrary line through Thrace, wherever drawn, would not have offered this advantage—and Philip's intrigues after the Peace of Phoenice had warned the Senate of the danger of such lines.

Antiochus rejected these terms, and the resulting war showed the Senate that the traditional policy of the small "free" allies was not enough, especially if these allies were politically conscious Greeks: they would not always be satisfied with the position of Saguntum and the Illyrians, and even at the best they would, in case of conflict, be content to become *praemia uictoris*. Thus the method was adapted, perhaps under the influence of experience gained in the Hannibalic War, and beyond the free states of European Greece there was created the great free kingdom of the Attalids, combining for Rome the known advantages of the "free" friend with the new advantages of strength sufficient to be of independent military value, but not sufficient to be able to cut itself loose entirely from the Roman connexion. Roman diplomacy had learnt its lessons well. It was twenty years before this new policy failed.

TENNEY FRANK (1876–1939) was perhaps the dean of
Roman historians in the United States in his generation.
As professor of Latin at Johns Hopkins University in
Baltimore he trained students in philology, epigraphy, and
history. An acknowledged expert on Roman economic
history, he inspired and edited the multivolume work, *An
Economic Survey of Ancient Rome,* himself contributing the
volume on Rome and Italy in the Republic. His book on
Roman Imperialism remains a standard work on the subject.
In this selection he seeks to explain Rome's actions in
Spain as a response to the peculiar character of the area
and the people, which forced on Rome attitudes and
behavior she did not exhibit elsewhere.*

Tenney Frank

Reaction to Spanish Treachery

Spain, apparently, had the faculty of
laying bare the worst flaws of senatorial
rule. This province had been acquired
from Carthage by the Second Punic war
and had been brought into tolerable order
during the stern but able governorship of
Cato in 195. In 179 Tiberius Gracchus carried the work of pacification to a more enduring stage by meting out rewards as
well as punishments and arranging a series
of compacts that were satisfactory to the
natives. For twenty-five years the province
prospered and enjoyed peace under his
settlements. Unfortunately, some of the
succeeding governors imposed unjust burdens upon the province. The tribute in
Spain, which was only one-half the usual
provincial tithe, was collected by the na-

tives themselves, but it seems that the governors were prone to go beyond their
rights in estimating the amount and in
sending officers to collect it. In 171 the
Spaniards sent envoys to the senate, re-
questing that the old methods be adhered
to. The senate promised to correct the
abuses of the governors, and peace continued till about 154. Then came some misunderstanding about the right of certain
Spanish towns to build fortifications, and a
distressing war resulted. This war was apparently near an end in 151 when Lucullus arrived. He, it is charged, through
greed for booty and a desire for a triumph,
attacked an innocent tribe on flimsy pre-
texts and broke faith with the people after
they had surrendered. Galba, during the

*From Tenney Frank, *Roman Imperialism* (London: Macmillan & Co. Ltd., 1914), pp. 230–233. Reprinted
by permission of Macmillan & Co. Ltd. Footnotes omitted.

same year, was accused of even worse treachery, and, in fact, was brought to trial at Rome by Cato, but escaped punishment because of political influence. After such deeds as these it is not surprising that the revolt spread widely. The contest dragged on for about twenty years. At times the Romans displayed good generalship, but its effect was offset by the blunders of several inefficient and dishonest men. Fabius, in 140, saved his army from slaughter by signing a disgraceful treaty; Servilius, in 139, secured the death of his worthy opponent, Viriathus, by a bribe; Mancinus, in 136, marched into a trap, and then saved the lives of his soldiers by a treaty promising independence to Numantia. The crowning disgrace, however, rests upon the senate, which refused to ratify Mancinus' terms, and, in order to escape the vengeance that falls from heaven upon the violators of an oath, delivered up Mancinus to the enemy, stripped and bound, but forgot to surrender the advantages it had gained by the treaty. The war was finally brought to a close by the younger Africanus in 133, and the province started on the road to the great prosperity it enjoyed in Augustus' day.

Such is the unpleasant story that Appian tells regarding Rome's rule in Spain. To be sure, our source is not wholly reliable, but, after all possible allowances have been made, we must still conclude that the history of Spain between 150 and 135 reveals an unspeakable amount of inefficiency and treachery. The lack of success is partly accounted for by the fact that Romans of reputation avoided the province as unprofitable and difficult, and partly by the fact that the senate never fully realized the seriousness of the contest there. The treachery, of course, deserves no excuse, but it may perhaps be in place to consider why the Roman character developed its worst traits in Spain. The Ro-

mans regularly spoke of the Spaniards as peculiarly treacherous peoples. Now it is quite conceivable that the rules of the game were not the same in the ancestral customs of Spain and of Rome. Such differences often preclude an intelligent appreciation of an opponent's real temperament, and they alone would be sufficient to give rise to misunderstandings and charges of dishonesty. But it must be remembered that in facing the conquering Romans the defeated tribes allowed themselves the privilege of breaking treaties. It is natural, and has always been natural, for weak tribes, when compelled to surrender before the irresistible power and superior diplomacy of a strong nation, to sign the articles of submission with a mental reservation. They feel, and justly, that theirs was never a fair chance. They are in the position of an individual who has signed a contract under compulsion. The law does not support such a contract in the case of the individual, and the conscience of the native is quite logical in not demanding adherence to such a contract in the case of the tribe. For this reason, if for no other, the Spanish tribes constantly disregarded their oaths and treaties, and thereby gained the reputation at Rome of being peculiarly deceitful. Obviously, this condition must have reacted upon the generals who carried on the wars of the sovereign people. They learned to fight the native with his own weapons. They, too, when driven into close quarters, made treaties with mental reservations. The history of our wars with the Indians, and of the British conquests in East India, will sufficiently illustrate this tendency and explain some of the ugly facts of the Spanish period that we are considering. In the Italian wars of the fourth century the opponents had been on very nearly the same plane of civilization, and the customs of war were then practically the same on both sides. Hence, we hear little of such charges from either contestant at that time. In Spain, on the contrary, vital differences existed. The deterioration in the character of Roman diplomacy and warfare that Polybius noticed in his later days is traceable in some degree to this reaction of the barbarian methods of warfare upon Rome's armies.

There was also another cause for misunderstanding which the later Roman historian did not always appreciate. During the second century the senate had become so powerful that it asserted the right to revise or reject any treaty made by its general in the field. This, of course, was not the practice later: Sulla, Pompey, and Cæsar were so strong that they could compel the senate to ratify their arrangements to the last word. Nor had any such right been assumed by the senate before the Punic wars. The old consuls of the fourth century had employed the senate as an advisory body, but they were not compelled to submit their acts to it for supervision or correction. Whatever arrangements they made in the field were practically final. It is not difficult to see that diplomatic confusion must have resulted from the senate's encroachments upon the powers of its generals during the second century. The senate hardly dared reject the arrangements of a Scipio, to be sure, but, when a young prætor in Spain agreed to disgraceful terms in order to extricate his army from a trap, would the treaty be binding? The Spanish tribes probably thought it would be, since they were supposed to be bound by the pledge of their chief. The Roman general who signed for Rome may have felt that he stood on constitutional ground in binding the state. But for a few decades at least the senate, in the heyday of its power, undertook to assume revisory rights. To the senators it became a constitutional question of great importance whether the senate must not, whenever possible, support the new aristocratic theory of government and compel the general to submit himself to the senate. We understand, therefore, why the problems presented by the treaty of Mancinus were not easy to solve. Not only did differences in customs and practices of war make it impossible for the Romans and Spaniards to understand each other, but constitutional changes affecting the Roman senate made it difficult for that body to decide the fate of Spanish tribes on the merits of each individual case. In the end, Spain became the burial ground of Rome's pristine fame for fair dealing.

A. SCHULTEN (b. 1870), professor of ancient history at the University of Erlangen, is generally acknowledged as the foremost authority on Roman Spain. Schulten's volumes on Numantia, his contributions on Spain to the German and Italian classical encyclopedias, and his chapters in the *Cambridge Ancient History* are all fundamental works on the Roman experience in Spain. In this selection Schulten describes the progress of Roman rule on the Iberian Peninsula and the consequences in Rome of that expansion. His judgment of Roman motivation, brutality, and treachery is unqualified and harsh. The events not only reveal an unattractive side of Roman character, but dramatize the errors of a ruthless imperialism.*

A. Schulten

Roman Cruelty and Extortion

The conquest of the Carthaginian province in Spain had been a necessary step in the war against Hannibal, for Spain was the arsenal of the Carthaginians. In fact, with the capture in 200 B.C. of New Carthage, which was the great mining centre and storehouse of supplies, the resistance of the Carthaginians began to weaken. It is true that Rome might have contented herself with this acquisition, as Carthage had contented herself with the possession of the south and east. But such a limitation was not in accordance with the character of Rome, whose habit it was to complete what she began. Moreover the highlands, too, were rich in metals and therefore tempting to Roman greed and worth a strenuous effort. The

safety of the Roman province was not seriously jeopardized by the occasional forays of the mountain tribes, especially the Lusitanians. Carthage, after all, had lived at peace with them for more than 250 years (500–230 B.C.), for Hannibal had been the first to attack them, and he had done so, not in order to conquer them but to reduce them to quiescence before the outbreak of war with Rome. But Rome was determined to exploit the Spanish provinces (as she had exploited her earlier provinces, Sicily and the islands of Sardinia and Corsica), partly, that is to say, by the imposition of taxes, but also, in view of the notable military qualities of the Iberians, by raising levies of auxiliary troops. They had hitherto been recruited voluntarily, and for

*From A. Schulten in *The Cambridge Ancient History,* edited by S. A. Cook, F. E. Adcock, and M. P. Charlesworth (London: Cambridge University Press, 1954), vol. VIII, pp. 307-324. Footnotes omitted.

pay, but military service was now no doubt made obligatory.

We have no detailed information regarding the conditions under which the Iberian communes entered the Roman confederation, but, generally speaking, the expulsion of the Carthaginians simply meant that they became subjects of Rome. Special treaties would be made only with the larger tribal units, and to some of these the better conditions of the *foedus* would be granted, as was done to Gades and no doubt to the other Phoenician towns. In the internal affairs of the communes Rome intervened only so far as was necessary in her own interests, as, for example, in bringing together the inhabitants of the small and often petty strongholds (*castella, turres*) into towns. In Nearer Spain, out of 293 communes, there were still in the time of Augustus 114 rural communes (*gentilitates*), i.e. communes without an urban centre, especially among the Astures and Cantabri, but there were none in the rest of the peninsula. The coins which Rome caused to be minted name only towns, not kings or tribes. Moreover larger tribes (*gentes*) such as we find in Gaul scarcely existed as political entities. The chiefs (*reguli, principes*) were no doubt mostly done away with. When we find the Turdetanian chief Culchas in the year 206 ruling over 28 towns, but in 197 only over 17, it would seem that some of his towns had been taken from him, and that was probably a reason for his defection. In the same way a small community Lascuta, which had been subject to Hasta, was taken from it and made independent (*C.I.L.* II, 5041). The only form of political organization which Rome as a rule recognized in the communes was the Council of Elders, the primeval form of government among Iberians and Berbers. It is spoken of as the *senatus* (Livy XXXIV, 17). Any concentration of power in the hands of chiefs was unwelcome

to Rome, while, on the other hand, the looser form of government by the Elders was convenient, if only because it was a guarantee of separatism. Generally speaking, both tribute and auxiliaries would be demanded; and the Iberians no doubt accommodated themselves to these conditions with characteristic indifference. But it was not to be expected that the governors would content themselves merely with the legal imposts either in the interests of the State or of themselves; they were likely to proceed to further exactions, and herein they had to reckon upon an obstinate resistance. Besides, some of the Iberian communities made the Carthaginian cause their own, and from the first fought with determination for Carthage, or rather for their own autonomy. This was the case with two important towns of *Hispania Ulterior*, Ilurci (Lorca) and Astapa (Estepa); Ilurci was only taken after a desperate resistance, while the citizens of Astapa ended by flinging themselves into the flames which were devouring their possessions (206 B.C.). . . .

In addition to precious metals the Iberian communes had also to deliver other natural products, especially corn and perhaps oil. To collect the tribute *praefecti* were sent to the communes, a practice against which the Spaniards petitioned in the year 171 B.C. (Livy XLIII, 2). Apart from the fixed tribute a *vigesima*, or five per cent. tax, was levied on corn (Livy XLIII, 3), in connection with which it was customary for the Roman officials to settle the price, but in 171 the Spaniards protested against this procedure with success.

More burdensome than the high tribute were the extortions of the governors. In the history of provincial administration Spain marks an epoch, since it was the extortions practised there which caused the establishment and development of courts for trying claims for redress (*repetundae*). In the year

171, in consequence of complaints from both provinces, the first such court was set up, and in the year 149, after the outrages perpetrated by Lucullus and Galba, this court was made permanent. Livy (XL, 44) relates the highly significant fact that a governor, who in the stress of war had vowed games and a temple, wrung from the Iberians the means to perform his vow. Equally oppressive was the levying of troops, the scale of which is shown by the credible statement in ancient writers that the small tribes of the Belli and Titti in eastern Celtiberia had to provide 5000 fighting men, and that Scipio before Numantia had some 40,000 auxiliaries. If the Romans were at first welcomed as deliverers from the Carthaginian yoke, the Spaniards soon saw that they had only exchanged one master for another, and that the change was for the worse (Livy XXXIV, 18). A recent historian writes with justice "What the pages of the history of Rome in Spain down to the year 133 have to tell us, whether explicitly or implicitly, takes its place among the most shameful records in the whole of that history."

The few communities to which Rome had granted a *foedus* were, however, in a slightly better position. The Greek city of Emporium, which had long had an alliance with Rome, was allowed to continue to strike its own coinage, with Greek legends, upon its own monetary standard, and a similar privilege was granted to the Phoenician towns newly admitted to alliance, like Gades and Ebusus, which continued to use Phoenician legends. The Romans had every reason to treat the inhabitants of Emporium well, for it had constantly served the conquerors as a *point d'appui*. Here the Scipios had landed in 218; here, too, Cato in 195 when the whole of Nearer Spain was as good as lost. The only town with Roman citizenship was the colony of Italica founded by Scipio Africanus. In the

year 171 the Latin colony of Carteia, for the sons of soldiers who had taken native wives, was founded, or rather planted in the existing town (Livy XLIII, 3). The colony is further described as *libertinorum*, from which it appears that these people of mixed Roman and Iberian race did not become *peregrini* but freedmen. There was no *conubium* between Romans and Iberians.

In wealth the two provinces were unequal. Nearer Spain possessed great abundance of silver in the neighbourhood of New Carthage, but, apart from that, was the poorer. Further Spain had from ancient times carried on intensive mining operations for copper (Rio Tinto), silver (Sierra Morena), and gold, while the valley of the Baetis was very rich in wheat, olives and wine. As early as 203 B.C. great quantities of corn were exported to Rome (Livy XXX, 26). It is easy to imagine how greedily both magistrates and private persons flew upon these rich spoils—the sixteenth-century Spaniards in Peru and Mexico offer a parallel. The Roman annals tell us of the vast body of silver and gold which the governors brought to Rome. In the years 206–197 alone the quantities of bullion amounted to 130,000 lb. of silver and 4000 lb. of gold.

The figures cited below show that Further Spain provided much richer spoil than the neighbouring province. Livy expressly states that L. Stertinius, the praetor of Further Spain, made no claim to a triumph, so that he must have obtained these masses of gold and silver not as booty in war but by taxation and extortion. The outbreak in the following year, 197, of a formidable revolt which extended to both provinces needs no further explanation. Nor is it without significance that the revolt broke out among the unwarlike Turdetanians and that the wholly peaceable Phoenician trading towns of Malaca and Sexi took part in it. Indeed the fact that

Rome had not spared even these towns, with which it doubtless had an alliance as it had with Gades, is shown by the treatment of Gades itself, which in 199 B.C. had to complain that, contrary to the treaty, a *praefectus* had been placed over it. . . .

Between 179 and 154 there was respite from war, but as we have seen extortion continued. Finally, the Romans had to face new troubles. As on a former occasion, during the Celtiberian revolt of 153 and the following years a parallel revolt was running its course in Lusitania, though it was only occasionally that the military operations came into connection with one another. The Lusitanian War lasted uninterruptedly from 154 to 138, down to the death of Viriathus, the Celtiberian War from 153 to 151 and from 143 to 133. The Lusitanians in 154 B.C. struck the first blow by making a raid into Roman territory merely for plunder, not for freedom. In the course of this year the Lusitanians under their leader Punicus defeated several praetors, induced the neighbouring Vettones to take part in the war, and penetrated into the Roman province. After the death of Punicus the new leader Kaisaros inflicted on Mummius, the future destroyer of Corinth, a defeat in which nine thousand Romans fell. Kaisaros now sent the captured standards to the Celtiberians, by way of rousing them to take part in the struggle. This they did, but only till 152, when, won over by favourable treaties, they withdrew from the war. The Lusitanians next invaded the district of Algarve, the land of the Conii, and even crossed the Straits of Gibraltar and carried their ravages as far as Ocilis (Arzila), until Mummius drove them back. In 152 a new governor, M. Atilius, gained some successes, so that the Lusitanians made peace, but as soon as he had retired into winter quarters they broke out again. His successor Galba suffered a great defeat in 151, with the loss

of 7000 men, and fled to Carmona. Lucullus, from Nearer Spain, where peace had reigned since 152, came to his assistance, and won some success. Galba found a more excellent way. He induced the Lusitanians to submit, promising them land. When they had delivered up their weapons and had allowed themselves, ostensibly with a view to the settlement, to be divided into several bands, he surrounded them, unarmed as they were, and put them to the sword. Few escaped; but among them was the future hero Viriathus. We read that Galba retained most of the booty for himself. It was not for nothing that he had to stand his trial, and suffer the onslaughts of the aged Cato. . . .

The Iberians of the mountain country were ill-equipped for a war with Rome, for they were split up into a thousand communities of various sizes but all small, and not even those who belonged to the same tribe held together. In addition to this, they lacked that determination which gives staying-power in war, whereas it was just by her tenacity that Rome, in spite of all her defeats, had brought the war with Hannibal to a triumphant close. The highlanders' best defence was the nature of their country with its arid bare waterless deserts, its mountains and ravines which seemed as though created for the laying of ambushes, its extremes of climate, burning heat in summer and bitter cold in winter. To crown all, there was the great distance which separated Spain from Rome, making the conveyance of troops a long, arduous and costly undertaking. . . .

When the new consul, Lucullus, arrived in 151 he found peace already established. The raising of his army had caused hardship; it had been necessary owing to popular pressure to take the soldiers by lot and to reduce the period of service to six years. Scipio Aemilianus offered to accompany the expedition as a volunteer. Henceforward he dominated the Spanish war, which he made his own personal concern and conducted with the same success as his great ancestor. Lucullus, instead of returning home, attacked the Vaccaei and treacherously gained possession of the town of Cauca, where he ordered an indiscriminate massacre; but he failed in attempts on Intercatia and Pallantia, and so withdrew into Further Spain. Here he came to the assistance of Galba who had been following his example in carrying on the war by means of treachery and breach of treaty. As we have seen, the setting up, in 149, of a permanent court to deal with extortion was a consequence of the shameful actions of Lucullus and Galba. . . .

Popillius enjoyed no greater success in his attack upon Numantia (139–138). The crowning disgrace however was reached under his successor Mancinus in 137 B.C. After a succession of defeats he retreated hastily towards the Ebro, but before he could reach it he was surrounded, in the neighbourhood of Nobilior's former camp, and surrendered with 20,000 men. Tiberius Gracchus, the future tribune, made himself responsible for the fulfilment of the terms, since the Numantines were prepared to trust his word for his father's sake. But this treaty, too, the Senate broke, chiefly owing to the influence of Scipio. The capitulation of Mancinus was perhaps the bitterest disgrace in the whole of Roman military history—the surrender of 20,000 men to between 8000 and 4000. The breaking of this treaty and Scipio's part therein gave rise to lasting enmity between him and his brother-in-law Gracchus.

For the Senate to hand over Mancinus, as it did, was sheer mockery, a fine exchange for the army whose fate the Iberians had held in their hand, but whom they had foolishly let go, like Viriathus four years before. The generals who followed did not venture to attack the Numantines at all, contenting themselves with plundering the Vaccaei. At length, in 135, popular insistence secured the sending to Spain of Scipio, the conqueror of Carthage.

When he arrived in Spain, in the middle of the year 134, Scipio's first task was to restore to the thoroughly demoralized army some semblance of efficiency and military spirit; but in this he was only partially successful. With such troops it was useless for Scipio to think of attempting to carry Numantia by assault, and he made up his mind from the first to blockade it and reduce it by starvation. In the end hunger did its work. After Scipio had repulsed a last attempt of the Numantines to obtain honourable terms, and the besieged had finally been driven even to cannibalism, a great number of them took their own lives, and the rest laid down their arms. Fifty were chosen to adorn their conqueror's triumph. Thus Numantia, after a heroic resistance, had been overcome, not by the sword but by famine. Without waiting to ask the Senate's permission, Scipio burnt to the ground the valiant town which, with 4000 men, had defied 60,000. In the following year (132 B.C.) he celebrated his triumph for the taking of Numantia, and assumed the cognomen of Numantinus.

So ended the last Celtiberian war, after a duration of ten or—if we reckon, like Polybius, from 153—of twenty years, and the loss of enormous numbers of troops. These great losses did much to give an impulse to the reforms of Tiberius Gracchus, who sought by increasing the numbers of the farming class to increase the number of those qualified to serve in the army. But even apart from this, the war bit deep into the life of the Roman state. In particular it was responsible for exceptional laws, as when the ten years interval between consulships had to be dispensed with, as for Marcellus, or the prohibition to re-election to the consulship waived in favour of Scipio. It led, further, to the beginning of the official year with the first of January instead of the first of March (so that the time at which Europe to-day begins its year may be called a by-product of the Celtiberian War). As we have seen, the establishment of a permanent court to deal with extortion falls within the period of this war and followed the outrages of Lucullus and Galba. The constant ill-success of the ruling oligarchy resulted in an increase of the power of the people who were able to insist on the use of the lot in the raising of levies and the reduction of the period of service to six years. Again, instead of the assignment of the provinces by lot as was usual, Spain was assigned to Scipio in 135 by the decision of the people, and it was the people who insisted on waiving the existing constitutional safeguards in favour of Marcellus and Scipio. On the other hand the war also prepared the way for the coming of the monarchy. The holding of commands for several years and the maintenance of a standing army were all steps towards it. There was something not a little monarchical about the position of Scipio. From 145 onwards most of the generals in Spain were chosen from his family or friends, he surrounded himself with a body-guard (from which arose the *Cohors Praetoria*), it was to him personally that the rulers of the east sent reinforcements, and he took it upon himself to destroy Numantia without consulting the Senate at all. If he had been bolder or less scrupulous the monarchy might have come from Spain in 133 instead of from Gaul in 49, for, when Scipio returned to Rome as her deliverer, no element was lacking but his own resolve to be monarch.

After the conclusion of the wars with the Lusitanians and Celtiberians Rome remained in undisturbed possession of the Spanish provinces, and could carry on with still greater thoroughness that exploitation of their resources which had begun earlier. The most valuable accession to the State property was the mines, which passed over from the possession of Carthage to that of Rome. Later, many of the mines were sold, and we have bars of lead dating from as early as the second century B.C. which bear the stamp of private owners. Only the gold mines seem to have been reserved for the State. In the period of the Empire private mines were again taken over by confiscation, and Tiberius, for example, seized the silver mines of a certain Marius, from whom the Sierra Morena takes its name (Mons Marianus). In the silver mines of New Carthage there were, when Polybius visited them, 40,000 slaves at work. These mines occupied an area of 30 square miles, and brought the State a daily yield of 25,000 denarii. Posidonius paints in sombre colours the sufferings of the slaves who worked in them. Whether these slaves were Iberians or foreigners we do not know, but the probability is that they were Iberians, for the wars must have provided a multitude of slaves.

The collection of the tribute with the extortion which accompanied it was certainly no less cruel than formerly, when it had constantly led to insurrections. And in fact insurrection broke out again in 98 B.C.; and again later, when Sertorius became the hero of the oppressed; and yet again, in the Augustan period. If the State and its officials set themselves to suck the provinces dry, private persons were no whit behind them in rapacity. As everywhere, so in Spain, at least in the towns of the south and east, *negotiatores* must have settled with a view to exploiting the Iberians by usury. It is true that finance was not yet highly developed, but as the communes easily fell into arrears with the taxes, there was an excellent opportunity of making fifty per cent, as happened in Rome's eastern possessions. How far the Romans themselves at this time engaged in trade and industry in Spain we have no means of knowing.

In general the Roman rule in Spain can only be described as brutal. The Iberians were treated little better than cattle. That was a blunder, and cost the Romans much blood and treasure, which a more statesmanlike understanding of the character of the Iberians would have spared them. Gracchus and Scipio effected more by clemency than their colleagues by the sword—just as recently in Morocco we have seen better results obtained by politic lenity than by force. Iberians and Berbers alike could only be won over by showing them the advantage which accrued from the ending of their unceasing feuds and the introduction of order, while in general respecting their racial characteristics. But Republican Rome did not concern herself with the psychology of barbarian races. Augustus was the first to break with the system followed by the oligarchy, and with him begins an era of colonization and prosperity in the Spanish provinces.

Scholars continue to grapple with the problem of explaining Rome's behavior in Spain. One of the most recent and most perceptive efforts is that of A. E. ASTIN (b. 1930) who has been at Yale University and at the Institute for Advanced Study at Princeton, and who is now Professor of ancient history at Queen's University, Belfast. Astin analyses Rome's policy in Spain in the light of her basic attitudes toward war and her system of military command. Rome's refusal to make peace except on terms of surrender was ingrained in her mentality and was a source of continual difficulty when dealing with a resolute foe. The problems were compounded by a system that lacked professional generals and relied on constantly shifting officer personnel.*

A. E. Astin

Foreign Policy Dictated by Structure of Government and Character of Generals

The Spanish wars, and their repercussions in the affairs of Rome, are not to be understood as the products of a policy of aggressive imperialism to which a policy of containment would have been a realistic alternative. They were rather the product of the very fact of the Roman presence in Spain, of the inherited situation, and of the desire of the Lusitanians and Celtiberians to modify that situation. The Romans could have avoided war only by yielding some measure of Roman authority, and it would never have occurred to the senators, or probably to the masses, that they should do this. There is no sign whatsoever that the alternatives of expansionism or containment were ever an issue in respect of these wars, nor is there reason to expect them to have been; the Romans simply did not think of these struggles in such terms.

Similarly, although the great length of the wars was injurious to the existing fabric of Roman society, by and large they were not prolonged because of insistence on a severe policy when a practicable alternative was available. An earlier termination of hostilities on a more moderate basis was scarcely ever a realistic possibility. It was excluded by the background to the wars themselves, by the presuppositions which governed Roman thinking, and by the long series of failures and defeats which were humiliating and galling, yet did not

*From A. E. Astin, *Scipio Aemilianus* (Oxford: The Clarendon Press, 1967), pp. 155–160. Reprinted by permission of The Clarendon Press. Footnotes omitted.

correspond to the true power-relationship of the contestants. This is true of most of the Viriatic war and of the whole of the Numantine war after about 142.

It might be objected that insistence on the *deditio* of the Numantines did prolong the war unnecessarily, since the Numantines were willing to negotiate terms as early as 139. Viewed in the abstract this is so; but the point is that in Roman eyes a negotiated settlement was simply not a realistic possibility. Once the Numantines had repudiated the agreement of *c.* 142, the Romans could not be expected to contemplate anything but a *deditio* (unless, of course, they proved physically incapable of achieving this, which possibility probably never occurred to them). The issue of the war had now become not merely the reassertion of Roman authority over Numantia but the maintenance of Roman military prestige. The policy seems to have been uncontroversial and taken virtually for granted. And once the decision had been taken, the ending of hostilities on any terms short of a *deditio* would have seemed a partial defeat; every extra year of war, every reverse, can only have deepened Roman determination.

Again, it might be objected that the policy of insisting upon a *deditio* was placed at issue in 137–136, when the *foedus Mancinum* was under discussion. At that time there was a direct choice of rejecting or accepting a treaty, and a treaty which was probably not unduly objectionable in its actual terms; and there was a group pressing for ratification of this treaty. But this pressure came from those whose personal prestige was at stake, and others did not share this basic motive. In the light of the circumstances and of the policy which hitherto had been taken virtually for granted, it is not hard to understand how ratification would have seemed to a large majority to be unreasonable and even outrageous. It would have been an admission of defeat not only in this one campaign but in relation to an established objective of the whole war; and that this would have been so was implied even in the arguments of Mancinus and his associates. Furthermore, for these very reasons, even in the very unlikely event of ratification, it is very difficult to believe that this would have achieved more than a short respite in hostilities.

There was one occasion when there was a real possibility that a less bellicose policy might have been adopted and that this might have mitigated the effects of the wars upon Rome herself. That was in 140, when the decision was taken to renew the war against Viriatus. Here again it is no surprise that Servilianus' treaty did not prove enduring, but it had been ratified and there was an obvious case for delaying resumption of the struggle until the Numantine war was finished. Resuming it at that particular time involved three or four more years of virtually inevitable fighting which had to be conducted simultaneously with the struggle against Numantia. It is possible that delay would have eased somewhat the strain upon Roman manpower and perhaps have avoided the crisis over the levy of 138. On the other hand, it does not necessarily follow that it would have been safe to reduce the size of the army in Further Spain even if the treaty had remained in force, and the potent political trends which manifested themselves in the dispute over the levy of 138 are apparent also in other events; so it is by no means certain that the decision to renew the Viriatic war added very greatly to the deleterious consequences of the Spanish wars as a whole.

At no other time was there any possibility that greater moderation on the part of the Romans would reduce the duration of the Viriatic war. It has been observed earlier in this chapter that in general Roman policy was relatively moderate and that the military situation virtually precluded any settlement for the first seven years. Once fighting had been resumed in 140, the struggle against Viriatus and his immediate followers did not last very long and could not have been curtailed significantly. Even if Popillius had offered more lenient terms in 139, this would have made a difference of only a few months. Brutus perhaps engaged in more extensive warfare than was strictly necessary, but even so he cannot have prolonged hostilities by a great deal; and his co-operation in the attack on the Vaccaei, which seems to be the clearest instance, was an unauthorized venture which met with official disapproval.

Within the context of the Roman objectives, which in general could not have been other than they were, the reasons for the length of the wars were the difficulty of the terrain, the remarkable resilience of the enemy, and Rome's failure to apply her full potential strength quickly and consistently, a failure which manifested itself particularly in the mediocre performance of several commanders and in the consequent demoralization of the armies. This failure could have been rectified in two ways: first by a much more massive military effort; but that would have increased enormously the immediate strains imposed on man-power and resources, and thus might have done nothing to mitigate the repercussions of the wars; second, by much more efficient generalship, such as if the commanders throughout had been of the calibre of Metellus Macedonicus or Scipio Aemilianus; but that is equivalent to saying that the wars could have been shortened and the strains eased if Rome had

had a totally different structure of government and military command, or alternatively if she had been unusually fortunate in the talents of the consuls of those years.

The conclusion stands then. Underlying the policies pursued in the Spanish wars were attitudes of mind which were largely taken for granted. Given these attitudes, together with the actual military situations, more moderate policies could not have been seriously contemplated; nor, within the established system, could anything else have been done which would have both shortened the wars and mitigated the strains they imposed upon Rome. It follows that responsibility for what happened cannot properly be attributed to any one political group or personality, and that it is misleading to single out Scipio Aemilianus in this respect. It is quite true that his character and career suggest that he will have approved entirely of the policies pursued; it is true that he was ruthless in his treatment of Numantia, and that he played a major role in the episode of the *foedus Mancinum*, or at least in determining what should be done about those who had taken the oaths. It is even conceivable that he often took the lead in pronouncing judgement on the situations and in formulating the decisions, though there is very little evidence for this. The point is that there is no reason to suppose that the decisions would have been different if he had been entirely silent. And that is so not merely because in practice he rarely enjoyed sufficient political strength to dominate the decisions of the Senate, but above all because in general no other decisions could have been regarded as realistic possibilities. Furthermore, it has been pointed out that the one significant decision to which there was a serious alternative was the abandonment of Servilianus' treaty in 140; yet in all likelihood this issue arose only after Scipio had left Rome on his embassy, and when the decision was taken he was probably in Egypt or Syria. Thus he cannot have been responsible for the forfeiture of this one possible opportunity to reduce the repercussions of the Spanish wars upon Roman politics and society.

Those repercussions took two main forms. There were first the increased social problems and tensions, resulting from the long and unprofitable drain upon resources. And one source of these tensions, discontent with the frequent levies for service in arduous and hazardous campaigns, focused attention and concern upon the increasing difficulty of raising adequate armies—a problem which arose primarily from an obsolete but deeply rooted method of recruiting. The repercussions manifested themselves secondly in the disputes and conflicts of the Roman aristocrats. Not only were the Spanish commands and the prize of victory the objects of ambition, but in these years the reverses in Spain provided a good proportion of the weapons with which the politicians belaboured each other and exacerbated their rivalries. And if these conflicts were not about the basic issues of foreign policy or the objectives of the wars themselves, no more were they all the opportunist exploitation of superficial misfortunes, though no doubt there was plenty of recrimination of that kind. The major conflicts arose out of substantial crises in the wars themselves, crises in which the emotion and self-interest of individuals were deeply involved but which also concerned the prestige and fortunes of the state.

It was not inevitable that the Spanish wars should make such an impact, or at least that it should be so profound: in 147 the Lusitanians might have accepted Vetilius' offer of resettlement; Viriatus might have died several years earlier than he did; the Numantines might have carried through the agreement of c. 142, instead of changing their minds at the last moment; or the Roman magisterial system might have produced a few more commanders of above-average ability. But none of these things occurred, and thus the long years of warfare, with all their consequences, were all but inevitable; for, given the predisposed attitudes of the Roman leaders and the institutional framework within which they were working, they had very few opportunities—probably only one—to take a decision which both seemed a serious alternative and might have mitigated the repercussions. And so the wars dragged on, complicating social problems, heightening tensions, exacerbating personal hostilities, and thereby contributing to the development of a major internal crisis.

Carthage was utterly defeated in 202 B.C. Her conqueror had imposed a heavy war indemnity and strict limitation on armaments, but had left her technically autonomous. For half a century thereafter there was no overt Carthaginian threat to Rome. Yet in 146 B.C. Rome's forces wiped Carthage off the map and annexed Africa as a Roman province. The reasons for this action have long puzzled historians. B. L. HALLWARD (b. 1901), who contributed chapters on the Punic Wars to the *Cambridge Ancient History*, places this question in the context of Numidian-Carthaginian relations. Rome sought a balance of power in Africa, as elsewhere, and acted to prevent the absorption of Carthage by Numidia. Hallward was fellow of Peterhouse, Cambridge, and University Lecturer in Classics.*

B. L. Hallward

Prevention of Numidian Expansion

During the fifty years that followed the close of the Second Punic War the rulers of Carthage could boast that they were scrupulously carrying out the obligations imposed upon them by the treaty of peace, and that their submissiveness to Rome never wavered. The greatest and most searching test of their deference had been given when they evinced their readiness to punish Hannibal, but throughout their conduct was correct to a degree. After 201 B.C. a Carthaginian officer raised an independent revolt in Northern Italy; he was promptly disavowed and exiled by the home government. In the wars against Philip, Antiochus, or Perseus Carthage furnished naval or military assistance as an ally of Rome, and was even zealous to offer more than the treaty required, an offer which was always coldly refused: the Carthaginian envoy Banno could claim in 149 B.C. "We have fought with you against three kings." In 200 B.C., 191 B.C., 171 B.C. and again a few years later Livy records large presents of corn sent to the support of the Roman armies. In fact, it can hardly be doubted that there was no shadow of truth in the allegations of treachery which Masinissa made against Carthage in 174 B.C. and through his son Gulussa in 171 B.C. Charges of secret conspiracy with Perseus and the still vaguer statement that Carthage had decided to build a large fleet were inventions which the Numidian circulated at Rome when the question of his territorial acquisitions at the expense of

*From B. L. Hallward in *The Cambridge Ancient History,* edited by S. A. Cook, F. E. Adcock, and M. P. Charlesworth (London: Cambridge University Press, 1954), vol. VIII, pp. 471–478. Footnotes omitted.

Carthage was *sub judice*. For true to the terms of the treaty Carthage offered no armed resistance to Masinissa's spoliation for nearly fifty years, patiently submitting her wrongs to Roman arbitration until finally, exasperated into an attempt to defend the last of the Punic empire, she provoked her destruction at the hands of Rome. Revenge, hatred and fear had so swayed the Roman Senate that they had deliberately allowed the balance of power between Carthage and Masinissa to be destroyed until the very weakness of Carthage endangered the peace of North Africa and pointed the way to the formation of a Roman province. The final destruction of Carthage had become partly a matter of cold policy and partly the last desire of unsated revenge. But before describing this final act of the drama we must watch the growth of the power of Numidia under its able monarch Masinissa.

Masinissa was thirty-seven years old at the close of the Hannibalic War. Tall and handsome, he was endowed with astonishing and enduring bodily vigour. At the age of ninety he still mounted unaided and rode bare-backed, and four years before this one of his wives presented to him his forty-fourth son. In addition to the physical qualities which exact the admiration of primitive peoples he was gifted with great powers of leadership and insatiable ambition. His Numidian blood gave him inherited mastery of all the arts of cunning and dissimulation which made him an incomparable diplomat. Lastly a youth spent at Carthage had enabled him to absorb and appreciate the benefits of her culture and his marriage with the daughter of Hasdrubal made permanent the lessons of education. He was pre-eminently fitted for the immense task to which he devoted the rest of his long life. For he set himself to make a united nation out of the nomad

tribes of Numidia, to wean them from their barbaric predatory habits to a settled life of agriculture and to extend his kingdom until, as he hoped, it should stretch from Morocco to Egypt, embracing Carthage itself.

In the Second Punic War with Roman help Masinissa had conquered the Numidian empire of Syphax from Siga to Cirta, and in the years that followed most of the independent princedoms which surrounded this dominion were reduced to vassaldom. But the chief accessions of territory were at the expense of Carthage. To the peasants whom he could bring under his rule he offered more security and lighter taxation than his burdened and enfeebled rival, and his sway was commended by his dominating personality and a powerful standing army which numbered 50,000 when in 154 B.C. he engaged Carthage in war. But it is as the "agent of civilization" that his true greatness lies. He established his sons like barons in newly-won areas of nomad tribes and in this way spread the improved knowledge of agriculture from the centres to the most backward parts of his kingdom. Strabo's statement . . . that Masinissa "made nomads into farmers and welded them into a State" sums up a great achievement. With the rise of the Libyans a new and native civilization, based on a capital at Cirta and combining Libyan and Phoenician strains, had appeared in the Mediterranean world.

The treaty made by Scipio after Zama contained certain definite and certain indefinite territorial delimitations between the empire of Carthage and the kingdom of Masinissa. The first principle was that Carthage should confine herself strictly within the frontiers of her empire as it existed at the beginning of the Second Punic War. This frontier line was to a considerable extent marked by what were called the "Phoenician Bounds" comparable to the Roman Imperial *limites*. It was an enclave extending from a point on the coast west of Carthage where the lands of the Massyli adjoined, southward in a semicircle across the Great Plains until it rejoined the coast east of Carthage perhaps near the north of the Little Syrtis. But, in addition to the land within these Bounds, the treaty recognized the Carthaginian colonies and trade-marts westward on the shores of the Mediterranean as far as Morocco and eastward the region of the Syrtis, her richest province, known as the Emporia. Carthage was not to move outside these limits, whereas Masinissa might occupy within these same limits any territory which either during the Second Punic War he or his father at any time had occupied, or his ancestors had held previously. The clause, of course, was deliberately designed to provide a source of friction which would steadily weaken Carthage and strengthen the client protectorate of Masinissa. When it was made, Rome was not yet mistress of the Mediterranean and she saw her imperial interests best served by fostering rather than allaying dissension in Africa.

In the fifty years which followed the treaty Masinissa proceeded to filch from Carthage all her maritime colonies, the Emporia on the Syrtis and equally those westward from Carthage. In addition he occupied a considerable extent of territory in the interior within the "Phoenician Bounds." Carthage was forbidden by the treaty to wage even defensive war against her neighbour, and our evidence shows a succession of Roman boundary commissions sent to arbitrate after a *fait accompli* and always deciding in favour of the client king. The exact chronology of these commissions cannot be recovered with certainty, but their cumulative effect is plain.

It is sufficient to follow the events which finally exhausted the patience of Carthage and precipitated an open breach with Masinissa.

In the years between 160 B.C. and 155 B.C. a plundering expedition had been made by a Carthaginian officer Carthalo into the territory which Masinissa had usurped. Raid and counter-raid followed until a Roman commission was sent which returned leaving the dispute unsettled. Then Masinissa proceeded to occupy a district in the Great Plains between Souk el Arba and Souk el Kremis called Tusca. Commissioners headed by Cato visited Africa in 153 B.C., and again retired after finding the Carthaginians unwilling to be entirely submissive to Roman dictation. All the old hatred of Roman for Semite seems to have been roused in Cato's breast. He was now eighty-one years old, and on the voyage home this hatred crystallized into an old man's *idée fixe* that Carthage must be destroyed. It was an unreasoning passion which only later clothed itself in arguments of imperial policy and advantage. Cato must have seen how Carthage was bleeding to death, and even if he hated to witness the prosperity which still flourished beneath the shadow of the city, he cannot have believed that Carthage could be a serious economic rival to Rome, still less a political menace to the power that had struck down Macedon and set bounds to the power of Syria. His hatred did not at once sway the Senate, and in the following year (152) Scipio Nasica at the head of another commission forced Masinissa to give up part of the land which he had occupied. But in Carthage itself the last fifty years had taught some men to hope for something from Masinissa and others to hope for nothing from Rome; but to trust to themselves at the last. In the winter of 151–0 the leaders of those who wished to submit to Masinissa were driven into exile and took refuge with the king, who sent his sons, Micipsa and Gulussa, to demand their recall. The more democratic nationalist party refused to admit the envoys to the city and, as they returned, the general Hamilcar the Samnite attacked them and killed part of their retinue. War was declared, and Masinissa laid siege to a town called Oroscopa.

The Carthaginian army of 25,000 foot was entrusted to a Hasdrubal whom Polybius describes as "vain boastful and without experience in command" though he was to show energy and determination later in the siege of Carthage. He advanced and was joined by two sons of the king, Agasis and Soubas, who brought the invaluable help of 6000 Numidian cavalry. Masinissa withdrew slowly into a broad plain flanked by steep rocky hills to force an engagement. Both armies had meanwhile been swelled by fresh levies until each numbered nearly 60,000 men. Scipio Aemilianus arrived from Spain on an embassy to procure elephants the day before the battle, and in later times recounted how like Zeus on Ida or Poseidon on Samothrace he had witnessed the struggle in the plain. The battle lasted till nightfall ending in a slight advantage to Masinissa. The Carthaginians, learning of Scipio's presence, called upon him to effect a settlement, offering to renounce all claim to the country of the Emporia and to pay 1000 talents indemnity. But negotiations broke down when they refused to hand over the Numidians who had deserted to them. Scipio returned to Spain with his elephants and meanwhile Masinissa drew a line of entrenchments round the Punic army and so cut them off from all supplies. Pestilence broke out in their army and, reduced to desperate straits, unable either to bury or to burn the dead and having eaten all their horses and transport animals, they

surrendered and promised to pay 5000 talents in fifty years. As the survivors marched out with a single garment apiece, Gulussa took his revenge and fell upon them with his cavalry. Only a very small remnant returned from this disastrous expedition.

As a result of his victory Masinissa was confirmed in the possession of a considerable additional amount of disputed territory. The later Roman province of Africa had the same boundaries marked out by the "fossa regia" as the realm of Carthage at the commencement of the Third Punic War. The limits have been in part determined by the finding of boundary stones, and for the rest reconstructed from literary and epigraphic evidence and Carthage is seen now reduced to domination of Northeast Tunisia and a narrow strip of coast line on the gulfs of Hammamet and Gabès. The Great Plains were in the possession of Masinissa and where the frontier crossed the Medjerda it was little more than ninety miles from Carthage.

Carthage had broken the Zama treaty by engaging in war without Rome's consent, and she had thus given an argument to her enemies in the Senate. On each occasion that Cato had spoken on a question he used his right to add one more sentiment to his *sententia*—ceterum censeo delendam esse Carthaginem. This simple formula he once illustrated by holding up before the *patres* a ripe fig, saying, "This was gathered at Carthage three days ago." There is no evidence that this act was an appeal for the destruction of a commercial rival—it was the excitement of Roman cupidity and revengeful envy at the fertility of North Africa. But besides these emotions there were reasons of State that had their force and plausibility. The balance of power in North Africa had broken down. Numidia threatened to absorb Carthage into a strong North African kingdom with an interest in the Mediterranean. A powerful Numidian ruling in Carthage might be a new Hannibal. The danger from Carthage was not that she was too strong, but that she had become too weak, and that her weakness might make Masinissa too strong. The last instalment of the war indemnity after Zama had been duly paid. This was an argument for the correctness of Carthage's behaviour in the past, but it offered no inducement to preserve her in the future. Such subtle considerations of callous self-interest, perhaps only half-avowed, reinforced the more respectable plea of ancient enmity and recent disobedience, and carried the day against the party in the Senate, headed by Nasica, who strove to save Carthage, as Cato himself had once striven to shield Rhodes.

When the Romans heard of the outbreak of war between Masinissa and Carthage they mobilized four legions. The Carthaginians realized what this meant, and after the disaster strove to show their penitence and obtain pardon. Hasdrubal and Carthalo with others who had shared the responsibility of the war against Masinissa were condemned to death, but Hasdrubal escaped and later managed to collect a force of 20,000 men from the outer districts of the Carthaginian dominion. Envoys came from Rome and enquired why these men had not been condemned before instead of after the war, and, when asked how Carthage could obtain pardon, they replied deliberately in vague terms that the Carthaginians must give satisfaction to Rome and they knew well what this must be. Rome was purposely obscuring her real intentions until her preparations were complete and by diplomacy Carthage might have been persuaded to render herself defenceless. Repeated embassies from Carthage to Rome were put off with the same obscure answers. Then after the consuls for 149 B.C. had entered

office Utica deserted Carthage and sent envoys to Rome, promising all the help she could give against her ancient rival. The news was expected at Rome, since Roman agents had been busy in Utica; the Senate met on the Capitol and declared war, entrusting the two consuls M'. Manilius and L. Marcius Censorinus with the conduct of the operations. They crossed to Sicily and thence to the base thus secured. The armament numbered four legions with 4000 cavalry, and together with a horde of volunteers who scented easy booty and a profitable campaign, may have numbered 80,000 men, as Appian says. There were fifty quinqueremes and one hundred smaller warships. The fleet was commanded by Censorinus, a man of quiet philosophic tastes, and the army by the orator Manilius. Scipio Aemilianus, aged thirty-five, was one of the military tribunes.

Meanwhile the Carthaginians, deserted by Utica and weak after their recent disaster, saw their one hope in unconditional submission and they sent five deputies with plenary powers. Arrived at Rome, they learnt that war had been declared and that the consuls had set out for Africa. They were informed by a praetor in the Senate that taking account of their unconditional surrender it had been decided to grant them "freedom and the enjoyment of their laws; and moreover all their territory and the possession of their other property public and private." These terms were granted with the reservation that the Carthaginians should send to Rome 300 noble hostages and should obey such commands as the consuls should impose upon them. It was ominous that in these vague terms there was no mention of the city of Carthage, but the envoys could do no more than return and procure the sending of the hostages to the consuls who had now arrived at Utica. Having dispatched the hostages to Sicily these delivered their next commands, that Carthage should surrender all her arms and war engines. Even these orders were promptly complied with, though it was pointed out that the city would be left at the mercy of the exiled Hasdrubal and his 20,000 troops; 200,000 panoplies and about 2000 catapults were handed over. When this had been finished, the consuls told the Carthaginians to send a deputation of thirty of their most important citizens to hear the final injunctions of the Senate. This body was chosen and sent and at last the consuls informed them of the will of the Roman people which had till then been kept secret. The inhabitants of the city of Carthage must leave their city which would be destroyed and could settle where they liked so long as it was at least ten Roman miles from the sea. At last the Roman intentions were seen in all their nakedness. Carthage had been disarmed, now came her death sentence. Once the fortifications had been pulled down and the superb harbour had been rendered defenceless Carthaginian territory would cease to have any importance if occupied by Masinissa. The inhabitants of a vast city were ordered to live or die without trade and without protection.

Two generations of scholars have received training and guidance from F. E. ADCOCK (1886-1968), professor of ancient history at Cambridge University. His numerous writings include books as diverse as *Caesar as Man of Letters, The Greek and Macedonian Art of War, Roman Political Ideas and Practice,* and *Thucydides and His History.* Even more important is his work as an editor and contributor to the *Cambridge Ancient History* and to the distinguished *Journal of Roman Studies.* On the Third Punic War, he stresses the irrational factor in history and Rome's groundless fear of her old enemy Carthage.*

F. E. Adcock

Fear of Carthage and Irrationality

The odious behaviour of the Romans in the events that led to the destruction of Carthage has earned the condemnation of historians who see in it, as they have a right to do, a moral issue. The unattractiveness of the Carthaginians, whose history has been written for us by their enemies, is no defence: the bad name does not justify this execution. But the problem remains why the Senate acted as it did, and the examination of it may throw light on Roman policy and the temper of the Roman mind in the middle years of the second century. We need not suppose that the Senate decided to destroy Carthage rather than listen any longer to Cato ending all his *sententiae* in the Curia with the words "ceterum censeo Carthaginem esse delen-

dam." The motives that led Cato, who after Pydna had spoken up for the Rhodians and apparently had quoted with approval a plea of Scipio Africanus against the destruction of Carthage after Zama, to urge the destruction of Carthage are part of the investigation. But the main question is why the Senate in the end adopted his policy, if policy it can be called.

The view, first put forward by Mommsen, that a guiding motive was the desire to remove a trade rival, has little to justify it. The fact—for it can hardly be an invention—that on one occasion Cato produced figs still fresh and declared they had been grown in Carthage, proved no more than the proximity of Carthage to people whose imagination needed that assistance. In

---

*From F. E. Adcock, "Delenda est Carthago," *Cambridge Historical Journal,* VIII (1946), 117–128. Footnotes omitted.

what had been Carthaginian Spain, Campanian pottery had found a market to the exclusion of Punic ware. Carthaginian goods were increasingly bought in the enlarged Numidia of Massinissa, but there is no clear evidence that when Carthage was destroyed Italian goods took their place. The Senate had during the last generation shown little readiness to be guided by the interests of overseas exploitation. In the twenty years that preceded its destruction, Carthage had imported ware from Campania and manufactures from Campania and from South Italy, but this would be a reason for preserving a good customer, if the Senate concerned itself with the interests of Campania and South Italy.

There were already Roman *negotiatores* in Carthage, but it is hard to see how the interests of Italian trade would be helped by the destruction of Carthage. There might be more grounds for supposing that the Senate had in mind the agricultural exploitation of Carthaginian territory for the benefit of the Roman landowning class, and some of the *patres* may have coveted African land, but the evidence points to little activity of this kind before the experiment of Gaius Gracchus. Polybius, who had ample means of judging the motives of the Roman aristocracy, gives no hint that any reason other than political played a part in the Roman decision to destroy the city of Carthage.

There was no real danger that Carthage would attempt to revive her naval supremacy in the Western Mediterranean. Her navy was negligible and was limited to ten triremes, and could not be increased without a direct breach of her treaty with Rome. In 153 B.C. envoys visiting Carthage had observed "vim materiae navalis," which should mean the raw material for a navy rather than a navy itself. It appears that the Senate demanded the destruction or disuse of this and that the de-

mand was obeyed, for when the Romans later demanded the disarmament of Carthage no mention was made of ships of war. It is true that it had become the traditional policy of Rome to avoid the need of maintaining strong fleets by preventing other States from having anything but very weak ones, but a State that could protect and transport a large army to Africa was too strong to be afraid.

A subtler hypothesis, for, in the default of direct evidence, it must remain a hypothesis, has been advanced, namely, that the Senate feared that Carthage would, by choice or under compulsion, become part of the kingdom of Numidia. If that happened, there would be a great power in North Africa, which would be dangerous for the Republic. The Senate therefore decided to forestall this event by destroying the city of Carthage. This hypothesis is seductive. The procedure of Rome was Machiavellian: it is attractive to assume that her motive was Machiavellian too, and what could be more Machiavellian than this? It is true that this motive is nowhere attributed to Rome, but the ancient sources leave much in darkness, and an *argumentum ex silentio* is not here apodeictic disproof. It is, however, not without significance that when Polybius recounts the criticisms of Rome's actions he does not include in them this artfulness, nor when he recounts the defence of Rome's action does he include the motive as revealing the far-sightedness of the Senate. There was certainly in Carthage a party that inclined to an *Anschluss* with Numidia, but the party was not dominant. It must surely have seemed to most of the governing class in Carthage that Massinissa could not be a friend and these would resent, rather than wish to emulate, the willingness which some Punic communities had shown to collaborate with Numidia. It would have been easy for the Senate to declare that any movement towards union with Numidia would be regarded as an unfriendly act, in essence a violation of the Treaty made after Zama. If the Carthaginian government decided to defend its independence against Numidia, as later its existence against Rome, the city's defences could easily repel the siege-craft of the Numidians. And Rome was not inhibited by Massinissa's past services from showing an interested benevolence towards Carthage which would immensely strengthen the anti-Numidian interest. Massinissa would not be the first monarch whose ambitions Rome had crushed without the need of moving a legion. It would be the traditional statecraft of Rome to check Numidian expansion the moment it seemed dangerous, rather than to create a vacuum which Rome's legions might have to defend. A Numidian king with Utica in his hands might prove a danger even if Carthage was destroyed, so that with the destruction of Carthage the danger would not be finally conjured. And though the old age of Massinissa was a "viridis et cruda senectus," and though he had recently become the father of another son, he was approaching the age of ninety. On his death Rome could be sure of a say in the succession and could, as she did, provide that the royal power was divided, wholly in fact and partly in form, between his legitimate sons, and that his illegitimate sons became the lords of fiefs held by the grace of Rome. The hard-won unity of Numidia in a single strong hand could be made of none effect, and it is not easy to believe that it was a part of Roman statecraft to force the issue while Massinissa lived, if it could be decided without exertion on Massinissa's death. That the Senate had on occasion succumbed to vain fears is certainly true; but that they did so now is not readily to be believed in the default of positive evidence. . . .

It has often been pointed out that the year 151 B.C. saw the last instalment of the indemnity imposed on Carthage at the end of the Second Punic War. The goose had laid the ultimate golden egg. This may be a reason why Rome did not move against Carthage earlier, and it might be a reason why Carthage should be brought under Roman protection and authority, at a price. For while the prosperity of Carthage had doubtless greatly fallen off since the year 191 B.C., in which she was able to offer the payment of all outstanding instalments, her resources were not exhausted. The goose in fact was still capable of producing eggs, if only silver ones. After the First Punic War, when the Carthaginians prepared to reconquer Sardinia, Rome had declared that Carthage was making warlike preparations against the Republic and imposed an additional indemnity of 1200 talents. When by opening hostilities with Massinissa Carthage could, with better reason, be declared to have broken the Treaty, it was open to Rome to claim a supplementary indemnity if she did not care to press the issue further.

If the above considerations are regarded as valid, then there appears, so far, to be no adequate explanation of the Roman decision not only to take action against Carthage but to decree the abandonment of the city, to be followed by its destruction. There is no hint in the tradition, nor any likelihood, that behind this decision lay any intention to convert Carthage into a Roman or Italian city. Had that been Rome's purpose it could, in great measure, have been achieved when the city was taken, for most was still undestroyed. The whole procedure that was followed, then, reveals the intention that the city should perish.

Before proceeding further it is necessary to state briefly and to elucidate the course of events which led to the actual beginning of the siege. The actions of Rome were in strict law not open to criticism. The Peace of 201 B.C. was broken when the Carthaginians began hostilities in Africa without the previous consent of Rome. This entitled Rome to declare a state of war whenever she wished and in point of fact she began in 150 B.C. to raise troops in Italy. The Carthaginians condemned the magistrates responsible for the war against Massinissa, but that did not repair the breach in the Treaty. Carthaginian envoys were sent, who in the end asked how they might obtain forgiveness. The Senate declared they must give satisfaction, but reserved their decision what the Carthaginians were to do. There for the moment the matter rested, while presumably the Roman mobilization continued. Then envoys came to Rome from Utica offering *deditio*. This was not the first time that Utica had taken this line. When Carthage had been hardpressed by the revolt of the mercenaries after the First Punic War, Utica had offered submission to Rome but it had been refused. Now that Carthage was in what may be called a latent state of war with Rome, Utica, which was a sovereign State, repeated the offer. It is conceivable, though nowhere attested, that she did this on the secret suggestion of the Senate, for her action set an example which the Roman government may have wished Carthage to follow without being prepared to indicate it in set terms. Whether this be so or not, the Carthaginians sent envoys to offer the *deditio* of Carthage.

It had long been known that by the act of *deditio* a defeated State ceased to have any right to limit the action of the victorious State. However much dictated by military or political necessity, the *deditio* was formally a voluntary surrender by a State of all its rights and the placing of itself in the *potestas* or *dicio* of another State. The State to which the *deditio* was offered was

free to accept it or not; by the acceptance the State did not limit the demands it might make on the surrendering State, and though it may have given assurances of its intention before *deditio* was made, these assurances did not constitute any part of a bargain which the *deditio* and its acceptance confirmed.

When the *patres* accepted the *deditio* of Carthage they imposed a condition that Carthaginians should do whatever they were told to do. It was clear that any failure would not restore to the Romans their freedom of action, for that they did not at any moment forego, but afford a legal justification for applying to Carthage the extreme rigour of war just as if no *deditio* had been made. The Senate's announcement that it would not take away the land, the freedom, the autonomy and the property of Carthaginians was only morally binding, and was that only inasmuch as the Carthaginians earned this indulgence by punctual and complete obedience to any orders given to them. The demand for hostages which followed was in accordance with practice, and so was the later demand for the surrender of arms. The Senate had said nothing about the city of Carthage. This in itself might not imply any intention of destroying the city. The Carthaginian envoys appear at first not to have suspected any evil, and the doubts of the home government may only have arisen in consequence of the formidable army sent to Africa and possibly some knowledge of the Catonian dictum.

In the case of Carthage no assurances of any kind had in fact been given before the offer of *deditio* was made, and anything the Senate may have said to the envoys from Utica about Roman intentions towards that community could not be assumed to refer also to Carthage. The sharpest critics of Roman action at the time as reported by Polybius could not assert that at any point Rome had acted beyond her strict legal rights or that Rome had broken any agreement by which she was legally bound. There was, it is true, a presumption that the defeated State, if it punctually fulfilled the demands of the victorious State, would suffer something less than the full rigours of war, which were not limited by any international convention. Otherwise there would be no point in *deditio*. Roman practice would suggest to the Carthaginians that if their *deditio* was accepted Carthage would be safe from being sacked by a Roman army as it might otherwise be—"urbes captas non deditas diripi"—and the inhabitants would be safe from enslavement, though Roman practice had admitted exceptions. The Epirotes had been sold into slavery in 167 B.C. But there the Romans had not made any announcement of their intentions, and even so their action went beyond their normal practice, except when provoked after the *deditio*.

The Roman Senate, ever ready to give itself the benefit of the doubt, was probably not at all conscious of having acted in bad faith at any point in these proceedings. No demand made by Rome on the Carthaginians, not even the demand that they should evacuate the city and settle elsewhere, was strictly inconsistent with the Senate's pronouncement what its intentions were if Carthage submitted to all demands made upon her. It is true that if Carthage submitted to all these demands, she was helpless; and no one can say what further demands might be made. But we have not the right to assert that these further demands would be inconsistent with the Senate's pronouncement. Had the Carthaginians submitted to all demands, they would, so far as anyone can say, have been left with what the Romans declared they would leave them. Autonomy and freedom and the possession of their private property might be secured to them even if the territory of Carthage became a Roman province. If they interpreted the Roman declaration as saying one word more than it in fact said, they were the dupes of their hopes, reasonable as their hopes might appear to them.

From all this it follows that the Romans were determined to destroy the power and the city of Carthage—"Carthago erat delenda"—but there is no reason to suppose that their intentions were to despoil the citizens of their private property, so far as this was not involved in the abandonment of the city, still less to sell the population into slavery: that is, the motive was not profit. This does not mean that the abandonment of the city would not condemn many thousands of Carthaginians to poverty, perhaps starvation. To very many it might be sentence of death: "You take my life, When you do take the means whereby I live." Vain as resistance was found in the end to be, it is impossible not to admire the Carthaginian refusal to see their city perish, as it is impossible not to condemn the Roman decision, as a moral, not a legal, crime. But the actual destruction of the city with the enslavement of its surviving inhabitants, once Carthage had decided to resist, was no more, though no less, than the enforcement of the utmost rigour of war as practised by the Romans and not by the Romans alone. The Romans were fully entitled to disregard their declaration of their intentions towards Carthage, once the act of Carthage had denied the premises on which the declaration was made. . . .

We may now turn back from the course of events which led directly up to the destruction of Carthage and consider the setting of Cato's pronouncements between his visit to Carthage in 153 and the moment not long before his death when his "ceterum censeo" had prevailed. After Pydna, the project was mooted of making war on Rhodes for her ambiguous attitude during the Third Macedonian War. Cato opposed this project in a famous speech, with the almost paradoxical candour that plainly appealed to him. Many peoples and States, he says, have feared "(ne) si nemo esset homo quem vereremur, quidquid luberet faceremus," and again "Rhodienses superbos esse aiunt, id obiectantes quod milli et liberis meis minime dici velim. sint sane superbi. quid id ad nos attinet? idne irascimini si quis superbior est quam nos?" And in the same speech he declares that the fact that the Rhodians "hostes voluisse fieri" is no reason for going to war with them. "Rhodiensibus oberit, quod non male fecerunt, sed quia voluisse dicuntur facere?" With this may be contrasted his words in what remains of a speech on going to war with Carthage. "Carthaginienses nobis iam hostes sunt: nam qui omnia parat contra me ut quo tempore velit bellum possit inferre, hic iam mihi hostis est, tametsi nondum armis agat."

This speech must fall between Cato's visit to Carthage and the Carthaginian breach of the Treaty of 201 B.C. Had it been open to Cato to point to a positive infringement of the Treaty he would not have needed to resort to the plea that Carthage was an enemy now because she was preparing to be an enemy hereafter. And it is to be observed that the Carthaginian infringement of the Treaty could not by any stretch of the imagination be described as aimed at Rome. That Carthage would have contemplated making war on Rome with Numidia on her flank seems to us incredible. Cato must seem to us to be urging a preventive war to prevent the impossible from happening. It may be in place to remark that Cato's earliest distinction had been won in the dark days of the Second Punic War, and in his old age fears

that had been real may have returned once more as ghosts mistaken for realities. The inexorable Clemenceau, even if inexorable with better reason, was a veteran of the Franco-German War. And if it could be believed that Carthage was to become dangerous, her proximity to Italy added to the danger. It was this proximity that was underlined by the episode of the fig, for it was its freshness not its commercial value that Cato invited the Senate to have in mind. When he pleaded for Rhodes, he was pleading for a State that was perhaps as powerful then as Carthage was in 153 B.C., but was distant, and he may have been rationalizing his *volte face* to himself and to others.

The first response to the arguments of Cato was one not unfamiliar, the sending of a fact-finding commission which took occasion to arbitrate a dispute between Massinissa and Carthage in a way favourable to Carthage. This would be the traditional policy of Rome, to mediate and at the same time to lean towards the weaker side, the policy which had for so long served the Republic well. Massinissa, of course, used his influence among Roman senators to stress the military preparations which Carthage was making against him, and in 151 B.C. there seems to have been a compromise reached in the Senate. The Senate apparently followed the lead of Scipio Nasica Corculum, who declared "nondum sibi iustam causam belli videri. placuit ut bello abstinerent, si Carthaginienses classem exussissent et exercitum dimisissent; si minus, proximi consules de bello Punico referrent." This implies that Carthage had not yet violated the Treaty of 201 B.C. and that the charge that she was preparing to violate it by maintaining a fleet alleged to exceed her rights by treaty must be met and that Carthage must demobilize, but that if this happened there would not be war. The Senate did not accept the plea of

Cato and other *principes* that Rome should send an army to Africa at once. So far it was a victory for traditional Roman policy, but those who had a set purpose of destroying Carthage might take some comfort in the *sententia* of Scipio Nasica: "nondum sibi iustam causam belli videri," which is one of those phrases by which compromises are reached by the use of words which mean more or less to one set of disputants than to another. If Carthage afforded Rome "iusta causa belli"—which implies a legitimate *casus belli*—Scipio and those who supported him would not be able, even if they wished, to vote against war. On the other hand it is inconsistent with a decision to make war whatever happened. Carthage promptly supplied the "iusta causa belli" by beginning hostilities in Africa without first gaining Rome's consent. The Carthaginians were defeated by Massinissa, and their field army was destroyed. While Carthage had ceased to be a potential danger, at least for the time, she was no longer protected by the Treaty of 201 B.C. It would appear that it was now, in 150 B.C., that Cato, and those who felt with him, were able to make the plea "delendam esse Carthaginem" prevail, though the decision was kept a secret; and Scipio Nasica must now have used his final argument that it was salutary for Rome that Carthage should continue to exist as a potential danger. The implications and the philosophy of government that attached, or were attached, to this doctrine have been admirably discussed by Professor Gelzer. The immediate effect was to turn against Cato the very arguments he had used in pleading against war with Rhodes and the argument which apparently Cato then quoted with approval as being used by Scipio Africanus after Zama. It was, speaking in a paradoxical form, the voice of traditional Roman statecraft of the old school, the notion that Rome was to be great by being the strongest of powerful States, which was really a policy of the balance of power. But the plea had a fatal weakness, fatal to Carthage. If Carthage was formidable, would it not be better to remove the danger rather than be schooled by it, and to remove it once for all? By alleging what seems beyond belief, that Carthage was formidable, Nasica did Carthage the worst of turns, and before Cato died his inconsistency had not hindered the triumph of his hatred. . . .

Polybius gives the formal defence of the apologists for Rome, but these do not touch the heart of the matter. On this we may divine the judgement of Polybius from two fragments of Diodorus to which Gelzer and Bilz have called especial attention. The doctrine is there enunciated that States win power by valour and shrewdness, augment it by reasonableness and generosity, and make it secure by terror and frightfulness φόβω καὶ καταπλήξει. Instances of the application of these various means are adduced from the careers of Philip II and of Alexander, and then Diodorus passes to Rome. "And they (i.e. the Romans) when they were practically omnipotent in the civilized world made their rule secure by terror and by destroying the most eminent cities." He then adduces the destruction of Corinth, Carthage, Numantia and the Macedonian monarchy. In view of the extent to which it is evident this part of Diodorus is based upon Polybius, it is highly probable that Polybius yielded to the temptation to defend Roman frightfulness by treating it as though it followed some kind of natural law. It is, in point of fact, an apologetic addition to the principle

> The same arts that did gain
> A power, must it maintain.

The elimination of the Macedonian monarchy might be justified by the growing power of Perseus that might mean a *revanche* and by the ancient prestige that attached to the Antigonid dynasty. The destruction of Corinth might demonstrate that the patience of Rome with the intransigencies of Achaean politics had its limits. Numantia had been at once a rallying point of Spanish hostility and the scene of repeated military failures. But Carthage had for half a century been far more assailed than assailant, and had shown no serious disposition to injure or even to resist Rome till the last spasm of despairing defence which followed the decision to end its existence as a city in its own right. And the destruction of Carthage did not daunt the ambitions of Jugurtha a generation later. "Delenda est Carthago," in fact, marked the advent of a phase of that irrational impatience that historians have, if reluctantly, to recognize as a factor in historical causation.

Few scholars of antiquity combined the scope, insight, and creativity of M. ROSTOVTZEFF (1870–1952). Born and trained in Russia, he left after the Revolution, already an accomplished and distinguished scholar. Yet his greatest years of productivity came in the United States as professor of ancient history at the University of Wisconsin and then at Yale University. Rostovtzeff has had no peers in his work on the social and economic history of antiquity. His mastery of epigraphy, archeology, and papyrology is reflected in numerous books and countless articles. His two-volume work on *A Social and Economic History of the Roman Empire* is a classic not likely to be superseded. In this selection he stresses the economic assets of the empire and the commercial and agricultural elements involved in stimulating Roman imperialism.*

M. Rostovtzeff

The Role of Economic Motivation

The basis of the economic life of Rome in the fourth century was peasant husbandry, a primitive agricultural system of life in which all the members of a family worked hard in the fields, employing in exceptional cases the help of some slaves, and of clients who from time immemorial were attached to aristocratic families by religious ties. Peasant husbandry and concentration on corn-growing were the main features of the economic life of Latium in general as well as of all the new territories of the new tribes (*tribus*) and of the new colonies, Roman and Latin, which were gradually included in the *ager Romanus.* Every new Roman settlement was a peasant settlement, every new centre of urban life, every new colony was a fortified village of peasants.

The little we know of the conditions in the uplands between Latium and Campania, in the Sabine mountains, in Umbria, Picenum, and Samnium indicates a close resemblance to those which prevailed in Latium, with a preponderance perhaps of tribal grazing over individual landownership and agriculture. The development of town life in these lands was slow, and it was confined mostly to the districts bordering on the territories of the Greek cities and the Hellenized cities of Campania. Even in Campania such a city as Pompeii, with its early houses of the atrium-and-garden type, was more a city of well-to-do peasants than of rich merchants and great landowners.

The greater the growth of the influence of Rome, the more extensive her con-

*From M. Rostovtzeff, *A Social and Economic History of the Roman Empire* (Oxford: The Clarendon Press, 1957), vol. I, pp. 13–22. Reprinted by permission of The Clarendon Press, Oxford. Footnotes omitted.

quests, and the more numerous her colonies, the more widely did peasant husbandry spread over Italy. At the same time the isolated centres of capitalistic husbandry decayed. The history of the Greek cities of Southern Italy need not be repeated. One after another, with few exceptions, they fell victims to their Samnite neighbours. Some of them perished; some—all the cities of Campania, except Naples and a few others—entered on a new life of Samnitic cities, that is to say, of cities of peasants like Pompeii; few kept their purely Greek character. The fate of the Etruscan cities after the Roman conquest is unknown. Most of them were colonized by Latin settlers; some probably lived their old life, the life of landowners and serfs.

The Punic wars on the one hand accelerated the decay of the few centres of progressive economic life in Italy and in the Carthaginian dominions (as well as in the Greek part of Sicily) and on the other enlarged the range of Roman colonization. Roman and Latin colonists spread to the former Celtic lands in the north of Italy; some went to settle in the devastated regions of Central and Southern Italy. The new provinces of Rome—Sicily and Sardinia, and probably also Spain—did not immediately attract large numbers of Roman colonists. They preserved the features of economic life that had prevailed before the Roman conquest. The former kingdom of Hiero was ruled in his spirit and by his methods. The Punic parts of Sicily, Sardinia, and Spain remained for the Roman state what they had been for Carthage— granaries and storehouses of various metals. In fact, as is shown by the picture given by Cicero, even the Greek part of Sicily was reduced by the Romans to the position of a corn granary for Rome. Notwithstanding the annexation of the first dominions of the *Senatus Populusque Roma-*

nus, the Roman state remained for a while a state of peasants. It was the peasant armies of Rome that vanquished the Phoenicians and it was the same peasants who conquered the East. The story of the Eastern conquests has already been told.

What were the economic results of Rome's victories over Carthage and the Eastern states? We must bear in mind that these victories were victories at once of the Roman state, that is, the peasant population, and of the military and political leaders of the state, who were members of the ruling hereditary aristocracy of Rome, the Roman senate. Being an achievement of the state, the victories meant for the state as such an enormous and steady increase in wealth. Besides acquiring immense sums of coined money and masses of precious objects in gold and silver, Rome became a large landowner. Vast tracts of arable and pasture land, forests, fisheries on lakes and rivers, mines, and quarries, both in Italy and in the former dominions of Carthage which were now Roman provinces, became the property of the state. The arable land, which accumulated gradually, was mostly divided among Roman citizens, who were planted out in new peasant settlements. Nevertheless, the increase in the number of Roman and Latin citizens did not keep pace with the increase of the *ager Romanus,* even in Italy, especially after the Gallic and the Punic wars. The foundation of new colonies was dictated more by political than by economic considerations. It is not surprising that most of the colonies were sent out to the north of Italy to protect the peninsula against dangerous invasions from the North: Rome never forgot the story of her capture by the Gauls, nor did she forget that the Gauls furnished Hannibal with his best soldiers. The south of Italy, devastated and decaying as it was, was less exposed to danger and, of course, less attractive to Roman and Latin settlers, except for Campania which, however, was only partially settled with Roman colonists and retained as a whole its Samnite aspect. We must assume that most of the cities of Campania remained faithful to the Romans during the Punic wars.

Large tracts of land, even arable land, thus became the property of the Roman state, not of individual Roman peasants. But it was not only the state that was enriched by the Punic and the Oriental wars. The citizens of Rome shared in the enrichment. The lion's share fell to the leaders of the Roman army, members of the senatorial class. From time immemorial they were the richest among the Roman peasants, like the corresponding class in the Latin and allied cities. During the wars of conquest they increased their wealth. Large numbers of men and cattle fell into their hands. When cities were looted, they had the larger share of the booty. They returned to Italy with their 'belts' (or, as we should say, pockets) full of money, and, if they did not dispose of them at once, with gangs of slaves and herds of cattle. Further, it was men of the senatorial class that were sent by the senate to administer the new provinces, the former dominions of Carthage. We have seen that these dominions and the Greek part of Sicily, the kingdom of Hiero II, retained their ancient status or, in other words, were regarded by the Roman people as part of their property, as their estates (*praedia populi Romani*). As conquered lands, they were ruled by military officers, magistrates of the Roman people, with almost unlimited power. The same system, as already stated, was applied to the annexed territories of the East. The government of the provinces thus became a new source of wealth for the senatorial class. Finally, by force of circumstances, by the fact of their growing wealth, this class was led to take part both in the credit operations which, as we have

seen were the natural consequence of the Eastern conquests and, despite a strict prohibition, in the commercial activity which followed from the concentration of capital in the hands of Roman and Italian citizens.

Apart from the senatorial class of Rome and a corresponding class in the allied cities of Italy, large numbers of Roman and Italian citizens shared in the profits which were derived from the dominating position of Rome in the civilized world. A large and influential class of business men grew up both in Rome and in Italy. Its members started on their career of economic prosperity by helping the state, including the allied cities, to exploit the extensive real estate which it owned—arable land, mines, forests, fisheries, houses, shops &c. During the period of the wars of conquest they supplied the armies with food, clothing, and arms; they bought up war booty from the state and from the generals, the officers, and the common soldiers; they sold various goods to the soldiers during campaigns, and so forth. When the wars were over, they used the money acquired by these activities to lend to the allies and vassals of Rome, whether kings or cities; they farmed the collecting of taxes and other state revenues in the provinces; they also settled down in ever-increasing numbers in the provinces, taking an active part in the highly developed business life of the East, as money-lenders, merchants, owners of land and herds, and proprietors of houses and shops in the cities.

Some of these business men never left Italy. Some went to the East, remained there for a long time, and gradually became absorbed in the local population. But perhaps most of those shrewd and energetic fortune-hunters, after having made their money in the East, returned to Italy and invested their capital there. When Sicily, Sardinia, and parts of Spain, Gaul, and Africa became Roman provinces, the Roman business men extended their activity to these provinces as well. The richest members of this new body of capitalists, the equestrian class, lived mostly in Rome itself and aspired to the honour of admission into the senatorial order by being elected to one of the magistracies. But the majority remained in their native cities, whether Roman and Latin colonies in Italy or Italian cities allied to Rome. There they ranked next to the municipal senatorial class, if indeed they did not form part of it, and, along with it, formed the upper section of the population.

The influx of money, slaves, goods of different kinds, and cattle from the provinces stimulated the economic life of Italy. The capital which was now concentrated in the hands of Roman citizens and of residents in Italian cities remained partly in the provinces, but mostly came to Italy. The majority of the new rich acquired their fortunes through speculation. Naturally, after gaining wealth, they wanted to find for it the safest possible investment, which would guarantee them a quiet and pleasant life in familiar surroundings. The safest investment which would secure an idle and pleasant life in the cities was landed property, the next best was money-lending and investment in Italian industry. This tendency on the part of the large capitalists was welcome to the state. We have seen that it now owned an enormous amount of real estate both in Italy and in the provinces. Unless these large resources were to lie idle—which of course was not in the public interest, when money was needed for public buildings, for aqueducts, for the construction of military roads, and for the public worship of the gods, including the games—they had to be exploited in one way or another. The only way was to attract private capital and to interest it in their exploitation. It is not surprising,

therefore, that the state encouraged the new capitalists to invest their money, above all, in the large areas of arable and pasture land which lay waste, especially in North and South Italy, after the horrors of the Gallic and Punic wars. There was no other means of bringing these lands under cultivation again. The number of Roman and Italian citizens resident in Italy and engaged in agriculture was reduced not only by losses during the wars but also by a steadily increasing emigration first to the East, and later to the West as well. There were no peasants available for settlement on the waste lands. On the other hand, there were large masses of slaves and there was a group of men willing to use them for the cultivation of the land. It is no wonder that the Roman senate gave these men every facility to restore the shattered economic life of Italy either by letting to them large tracts of land in the regular way through the censors, who had charge of such matters, or by allowing them to occupy the land informally with the obligation to pay to the state part of the produce of the land thus reclaimed.

That was the reason why in the second century B.C. a rapid concentration of landed property was steadily taking place. The landowners were either members of the senatorial and equestrian classes in Rome or the most energetic, shrewd, and thrifty of the residents in the Italian towns, whether allied cities or Roman and Latin colonies. These men never intended to take up residence on the farms and work the land with their own hands. From the very beginning they were landowners, not farmers, and therefore they swelled the numbers of landed proprietors in the cities to the detriment of the peasants, who lived in the country and were genuine farmers. The same class of men, on the other hand, by investing their money in industrial concerns and creating new shops and factories, which were run by means of slave-labour, revived the old-established industries of Campania and Etruria, at the expense of the small free artisans.

The members of the old and of the new aristocracy of Rome and Italy, most of whom had acquired their wealth in the East and had become acquainted with the capitalistic system which prevailed there, introduced this system into Italian agriculture and industry. They were aided in their efforts by the Greek manuals of scientific and capitalistic agriculture, which were translated into Latin from Punic and from Greek and thus were made accessible to everybody in Italy. We may safely presume that similar manuals existed for industry, manuals at least which aimed at making generally accessible the developments of Greek technique in that particular field. In the Hellenistic East capitalistic activity in the sphere of agriculture was concentrated almost wholly on the production of wine and olive-oil, the chief articles exported by Hellenistic landowners; good returns were expected also from scientific cattle-breeding; corn-production was left almost wholly in the hands of the peasants, who were either small landowners or the tenants and serfs of great landlords. It need not surprise us that this system was taken over by the pupils and heirs of the Hellenistic landowners, the aristocracy and the *bourgeoisie* of Rome and the Italian cities. These men applied the capitalistic system of management to industrial concerns also, especially in Rome, Etruria, and Campania.

For many parts of Italy the capitalistic tendencies of the second century B.C. and the introduction of Hellenistic methods into Italian husbandry were, as we have seen before, not novelties but revivals of ancient forms of economy. The development of the capitalistic system was facilitated by many factors besides the existence

of an ancient tradition and the fact that the rich natural resources of Italy made it a good field for the purpose. One of the most important was the abundance and the cheapness of labour. Enormous masses of slaves, mostly from Greece and Asia Minor, poured into Italy—they were partly skilled artisans, partly men who used to work on the scientifically managed estates of the Hellenistic kings and the Hellenistic *bourgeoisie*—and the stream never ceased to flow all through the second and first centuries.

On the other hand, there were now splendid opportunities for selling the goods which were produced in Italy, particularly olive-oil and wine, metal plate and pottery. The chief markets of Italy were the Western parts of the ancient world: Gaul, Spain, Africa on the one hand, and the North and the Danube provinces on the other. After the second Punic war Carthage was no longer the leading commercial power in the West. Her activity was confined to the improvement of her agriculture, especially to extensive gardening and the culture of the vine and olive. The heritage of Carthage passed to her ancient rivals, the Greeks of Sicily and of South Italy, now the faithful allies of Rome. The Eastern part of the Greek world, which was then suffering gradual economic decay, had no share in it. The destruction of Carthage completely and finally eliminated the Punic city as a commercial and economic power. Probably it was the Italian capitalists and landowners, led by Cato, who insisted on the destruction of the city. They were now large producers of wine and olive-oil, and they had every reason for endeavouring to get rid of a dangerous rival and to transform her territory from a land of gardens, vineyards, and olive-groves into one of vast cornfields.

We must not underestimate the importance of the Western and of the Northern markets and their purchasing power. Gaul was a rich country, very eager to buy wine and olive-oil and manufactured goods, which the Greek cities of Gaul and (in the last quarter of the second century) that part of the country which was occupied by the Romans did not produce in sufficient quantities. In Spain and Britain the conditions of life were almost the same as in Gaul. The ruling class in Britain and in part of Spain belonged to the same Celtic stock. The Iberian portion of the Spanish peninsula had been accustomed for centuries to Greek and Phoenician imports. Even Germany and the Danube lands became gradually acquainted with the products of Greco-Italian economic activity.

The developments we have described, which took place in Italy in the second century B.C., had far-reaching consequences for the political, social, and economic life of the country. Rome ceased to be a peasant-state ruled by an aristocracy of landowners, who were mostly richer peasants. There arose now all over Italy not only an influential class of business men, but a really well-to-do city *bourgeoisie*. In fact it was in the second century that Italy became for the first time urbanized, in the Greek sense of the word. Many ancient cities, partly Greek or Etruscan, enjoyed an unexpected revival of prosperity. Many towns, villages, marketplaces and hamlets not only received a city-constitution but also assumed the social and economic aspect of real cities. This was due to the growing importance of the already mentioned class of municipal shopowners and landed proprietors, who during their stay in the Hellenistic East had become habituated to the comfort of city life and had assimilated the ideals of the *bourgeois* class, and returned to promote city life and *bourgeois* ideals in Italy.

This new city *bourgeoisie* took no active part in the political life of the state. The leading position was still held by the Roman aristocracy. The *bourgeoisie* was too busy in organizing its economic life, and in building up the cities (such as Pompeii, with its beautiful houses of the Tufa period, adorned with artistic fronts and gorgeous wall paintings and mosaics) to aspire to any share in the public life of the capital. Moreover, this class was perfectly satisfied with the policy of the leaders of the Roman state. Their material interests and their political ideals mostly coincided with those of the Roman aristocracy. Like the members of that class, they generally invested their money in Italian lands, which were chiefly cultivated as vineyards and olive-groves or used as pasture lands. Hence the tacit support which they gave to the ruthless policy of Rome towards Carthage and to such measures of the senate as the prohibition of vine-planting in the newly acquired western provinces of Rome. Like the senators and the Roman knights, they also invested their money in vine and olive land in Greece and Asia Minor. Hence they supported the policy of the senate in the East, and had a large share in the financial and economic exploitation of the provinces in general. They were therefore staunch supporters of the government when it took the first steps on the path of imperialism.

The impact of economic considerations on Roman imperialism has been the subject of much scholarly dispute. The evidence is fragmentary and controversial. E. BADIAN subjects that evidence to a rigorous reexamination. In arguing against Rostovtzeff, as well as against Marxist historians, Badian revives the older view of Tenney Frank that business and trading interests did not on the whole influence the course of Roman foreign policy. He cautions against unconsciously smuggling modern notions into an ancient situation where they are not applicable.*

E. Badian

The Lack of Economic Motivation

In every society, there is inevitably a close connection between the values and way of life—the *Weltanschauung*—of the leading classes of that society at home and the way in which the society, as led by those classes, will act in its foreign relations. This is particularly so where, as in the case of Rome, a small and relatively isolated society has, within a very few generations, found its horizons vastly extended, almost to the limits of the civilised world of its time; and where, moreover, it has entered that world as a superior and a master, able to make others to a very large extent conform to its own patterns. . . . At a different stage of social and international development, the influence could go the other way and the relations of eminent Romans with most of the outside world could impose a pattern on internal relationships. But at the point we have reached that was still in the future, even though dimly visible. The constant interaction of the internal temper and customs of social life and the external environment of a society is an important and obvious field of study to the historian trying to evaluate both. Yet these aspects are often studied in isolation and thus individually distorted.

The modern student, accustomed to seeing history—at least at second or at tenth hand—through the blood-red spectacles of Marx, may by now have become impatient with my approach, observing that a discussion of Roman imperialism in terms of politics, strategy, social *ethos* and

*Reprinted from E. Badian: *Roman Imperialism in the Late Republic.* Copyright © Basil Blackwell, 1968. Used by permission of Cornell University Press and Basil Blackwell and Mott, Ltd. Pp. 16–21. Footnotes omitted.

even psychology, surely misses the point: what (he will say) about revenues, markets, exports? These (we are constantly taught) are the real stuff of imperialism.

This view is not confined to the student unfamiliar with the evidence. Variants of it have at times been propounded by distinguished scholars: we shall never escape contemporary fashions, and economic explanations of political events are commonly supposed to be one of the distinctively modern contributions to historical research. Yet this seems to me an obvious case where we tend to see history through distorting spectacles. I shall not follow up the larger question of whether such views, even in the case of our own society and the more recent past, tend to give an inadequate and distorted explanation of historical events: though I would not deny the importance of economic motives for political actions, it seems to me clear that this importance can vary considerably in different conditions and even in different cases, and that failure to recognise this, and over-emphasis on economic factors, has led, not only to many mistaken historical interpretations, but also to many wrong political decisions. However, our main point at present is that no such motives can be seen, on the whole, in Roman policy, during the period that we are now considering.

Naturally, we have one or two cases of economic privileges secured for Romans and Italians: the best-known is freedom from duty at Ambracia. There is also that old favourite of economic historians, the free harbour established at Delos in 167 B.C. However, those directly benefiting (particularly in the latter case) were not Roman aristocrats—though these may have got the odd slave a little more cheaply—nor even, to a large extent, Roman citizens: apart from numerous Syrians and other Orientals, they were Italians. Many of the "Romans" at Delos come

from Oscan Italy. The protecting power, acting in the true spirit of a patron, was mindful of *beneficia* to confer—at no cost to itself—on its loyal allies. For in Italy the freedom and dignity of the Italian allies—whom moderns sometimes still miscall the "Italian Confederacy"—had been mortally wounded by the Hannibalic War and the two decades of disturbances that followed. Roman arrogance and lack of respect for the independence of the allies—whatever their treaty rights—were becoming painfully evident. But the Senate as a whole, though it could not always control its members, and though it might at times not be unwilling to make Roman power perfectly plain in the Peninsula, carefully fulfilled the obligations imposed by superior *uirtus*. And the upper class of Italy was, on the whole, satisfied. There is no sign of serious discontent, no demand for equality (not to mention citizenship), until Roman demagogues, for their own purposes connected with internal politics, create it in the 120s. Had the Senate not fulfilled its obligations—on the whole—to its clients' satisfaction, the Social War would have come much sooner and would perhaps have ended differently. Politics and even economics must be seen in their Roman aristocratic context.

Strange as it may seem to a generation nourished on Marx, Rome sought no major economic benefits. In their four provinces, the Romans simply went on collecting—with as little readjustment as possible—the tribute those regions had paid to their previous masters, the Carthaginians or their own king. Even the methods of collection, left essentially unchanged, brought little profit to Roman *publicani*. Of course, the Romans were too prudent in matters financial to give up established revenues; but they kept them as much from inertia as from conscious choice, and mostly because the alternative was simply

conceivable. It is unlikely (as we have
een) that at this time any province was
ven paying its way, except for peaceful
nd prosperous Sicily. In Macedonia, in
67, the royal mines were for a time closed
own, to avoid throwing them open to Ro-
an speculators: the motive has been
uestioned and Livy arraigned; but since
ne fact can hardly be denied, it is difficult
> find any other plausible motive for such
thoroughly un-Roman action. The tri-
ute that the four regions of Macedon had
aid to their king was halved when they
ecame independent republics. Perhaps it
ould have been unreasonable to demand
ne full amount from those weakened
ates. But exploiters would hardly stop to
nink of this. In fact, the tribute was
erhaps imposed—as Frank pointed out—
> pay for the expenses of the war, which
ould not be charged to anyone else's ac-
ount: Rome had certainly come to feel
hat she should not, as victor, be expected
> pay for her wars.

So much for exploitation. The wars
nemselves, of course, were highly profit-
ble—especially the great Eastern wars.
fter the triumph of L. Paullus citizens
ad no more direct taxes to pay. Money,
aves and works of art poured into the
ity. This was the ancient law of war. No
ne would have dreamt of questioning it.
ut as we have already had occasion to
e, neither this nor anything else in fact
ade the Senate eager for great wars, es-
ecially in the rich East. The profits, when
hey came, were welcome and were taken
s a matter of course. But they were not a
otive for political and military action;
ey were not actively sought.

Finally, markets. In a well-known pas-
age beloved of economic historians, Scipio
emilianus is made by Cicero to reprove
he Romans for not allowing Transalpine
ribes to plant vines or olives, in order to
ake their own farms more profitable.

Rostovtzeff called this "a prohibition on
vine and olive culture in the Western
provinces" and seized on it as his crowning
demonstration of economic motives in
Rome's foreign policy as early as 154 (or
possibly 125) B.C. In fact, as Tenney Frank
had by then already pointed out, and as
Rostovtzeff would have seen, had he
looked again at the text, the wording speci-
fies the tribes of Transalpine Gaul, and
thus *excludes* the tribes of the other western
provinces—such countries as Spain and
Sicily, rich in vines and olives. What economic sense is there in that?

But there is, in fact, another consideration that damns this ill-conceived theory.
We must remember that the *Republic,*
where this passage occurs, has 129 B.C. as
its dramatic date. Now, Roman treaties
were kept in archives or even displayed in
public, and Cicero certainly had access to
the one that contained the provision he
here attacked. So would those who mattered among his audience. It is inconceivable that he should here be guilty of a
gross chronological blunder and refer to a
treaty that was in fact dated *after* 129: even
Rostovtzeff's alternative of 125 will not do.
Had Cicero made the incredible mistake,
his friend Atticus, that careful chronologer,
would have corrected it. A Roman aristocratic reading public did not permit the
sort of pseudo-history that an Athenian
orator could get away with in court.
However, if the treaty concerned was already in existence in 129, it must belong to
the campaign of 154—the only time before
129 when Rome had come into contact
with Transalpine Gauls to an extent that
could possible involve such treaties. This
campaign, as Tenney Frank stressed, had
been entered into at the appeal of Massilia;
and after its end, as far as we know,
the Romans, for a full generation, continued to have no interest whatever in
southern Gaul. They certainly did not own

an acre of it, or have contacts close enough to lead to differences of opinion; and so Tenney Frank's explanation of the treaty Cicero saw is inevitable: the term he objects to must have been included at the request of Massilia, which itself had both agricultural and trading interests, and in fact probably almost a monopoly of trade in the area. We must only note, for future reference, that by Cicero's day, when the actual conditions of 154 had long been forgotten, and men judged—as men will judge—the past by the present, the interpretation that Cicero gives seemed the obvious one. The passage, therefore, is valuable evidence on his own day.

The whole myth of economic motives in Rome's foreign policy at this time is a figment of modern anachronism, based on ancient anachronism, like so many modern myths about the ancient world. Though exposed by Tenney Frank long ago, it is still from time to time fashionably reaffirmed; but it should be allowed to die. We must add, briefly, that the destruction of Carthage and Corinth, sometimes cited against Frank's thesis, in fact confirms it: having it in their power to settle on those splendid commercial sites (as, much later, they did), the Romans preferred to plough them up. Their motives were purely strategic and political: to strike at strongly for-

tified centres of traditional anti-Roma leadership. We might compare the lon hesitation over the foundation of a settle ment at Capua.

In fact, the events of 148–6 show th Senate's traditional policy and frame c mind. Macedonia had to be annexed, afte controlled independence had turned ou disastrous: the Romans, on the whole, nev er made the same mistake twice. Th same—from the Roman point of view— applied to the small strip of Tunisia whicl was all that was left of Carthage and it empire. But Greece, despite all th troubles her cities had caused, was, for th most part, still not put under direct adminis tration; and a Greek—the historian Po lybius—was left to work out the details c the final settlement. In Africa, part of th small territory annexed was immediately handed over to the possession of loya allied cities that remained "free," i.e. out side the province. So little did Rome car about the exploitation even of land tha rightly belonged to her. (Or, if we prefer it so seriously did the Senate still take th duties of patronage, to the neglect o Rome's economic interests.) The policy o minimising administrative commitment and caring little for profit derived from provincial territories could hardly appea more clearly.

R. E. SMITH (b. 1910) is professor of ancient history at the University of Manchester. His principal contributions have been to the political and social history of the Roman Republic, as evidenced by his *Service in the post-Marian Roman Army* and *Cicero the Statesman.* Smith's book, *The Failure of the Roman Republic,* is a stimulating interpretation of Rome's gradually disintegrating moral and social structure culminating in the collapse of the Republic. In the chapter reprinted here he examines the failure of her foreign policy as an inability to accept moral responsibility for governing an empire. The critical question raised is whether a nation operating within the conventions of a city-state can adapt to the role of a world power.*

R. E. Smith

City-State Unable to Act as World Power

Rome was now the most important city of Italy, with which Latium and the rest of Italy were joined in a diverse system of alliances. This was the outcome of centuries of struggle, through which had slowly emerged by trial and experimentation this organization, an organization which had proved equally fruitful to Rome and to the constituent members. Rome and her allies had defeated the Carthaginians in one war, and in the aftermath had become possessed of the islands of Sardinia and Corsica as well as Sicily; in 200 B.C. she had just emerged from the death-struggle of the second Punic War, a war which had tested to the limit every link in the chain of her confederation, and in which very few of the links had proved

weak. The weak ones had been strengthened; Rome and her confederation could gaze with awe upon the huge giant which now lay at her feet, and which, in spite of the mortal terror it had at first created, in spite of the vast damage it had wrought throughout the length and breadth of Italy, now panted prostrate, awaiting the signal of the victor's thumb.

Rome had fought for her very existence; not surprisingly therefore in the treaty of peace she took stringent precautions against the resurgence of the military might of Carthage. Her commerce was left free; but her military strength was strictly confined. This was natural; Rome's position was not yet assured; her important wars had been fought in self-defence or to

*From R. E. Smith, *The Failure of the Roman Republic* (London: Cambridge University Press, 1955), p. 47–56. Footnotes omitted.

prevent others becoming strong enough to constitute a menace; and to her the Mediterranean world with its Hellenistic monarchies was an arena in which others could rise to threaten her security or existence.

Her experience with Carthage had made it clear to her that, as armies might march into Italy from the West, so they might from the East, and that as a seaborne army could be taken to and from Carthage and Italy, so could armies sail from Greece. The neutralizing of Greece was therefore her first concern. From the West she was secure; she must establish a similar security from the East. She did not want to possess Greece, nor did she feel towards her the responsibilities of a guardian; she merely wished to keep it free of any strong external state. The maintenance of Greece as a neutral zone, with her "independence" guaranteed by Rome alone was the cardinal point of Rome's policy during these years. Fears that it might be occupied by Philip V, Antiochus the Great and Perseus were chiefly responsible for her three major wars. She was determined to allow no strategic disadvantage to develop, and since Greece in the wrong hands seemed to present just that disadvantage, there arose what we may call this "preventive habit," which continued, as we shall see, when changed circumstances no longer required this precaution. The use she made of her victories acquits her of imperialistic designs or ruthless power-politics. The first two wars added not one acre of territory to her possessions; having contained these princes within their domains and having thus freed Greece from their activities, she left them free to pursue their ambitions where they would not worry Rome. Even when Macedon's independence ended, Rome made no effort to exploit the country; at first it was divided into four Republics, paying to Rome but

half the tribute they had paid their king, and only with reluctance did Rome assume direct responsibility for its government, when it would not be peaceable and hence became a source of worry.

Her attitude to and treatment of Greece itself well illustrate the limitations of Rome's outlook, which are to be discerned in all her foreign policy, and which were the result of her political immaturity. While Greece was wholly within Rome's orbit, Rome was content; Greece could live whatever life she chose, within her own confines in whatever system of leagues and alliances she pleased. Further, Rome wanted her to do that; she did not want and never contemplated, the assumption of any responsibility for Greece's government or her economic and social progress. Her interest was narrowly political, concerned only with Rome's security. Yet it was impossible to confine her interests within so narrow a compass; Rome's very shadow across their country displeased many Greeks; their social and economic problems were great, and it was not surprising that later on many Greeks, displeased that Rome interfered in their internal affairs without solving their internal problems, turned to outside help.

The natural consequence was further Roman interference, and thus relations continued to be bedevilled between the two countries. Greece was in fact not free, yet Rome wanted her to act as though she were, although to do so might well provoke Rome's anger. Rome could not see Greece's dilemma, because she was thinking only in terms of her own safety, and knew little of Greece's internal problems beyond the point where they ceased to affect Rome's safety. She did not see that social and economic conditions affected politics, and her own interest was strictly political; hence she could not see that she was denying Greece the right to live her own life, while refusing to organize it for her.

Yet we should not convict her of wilful irresponsibility. It was the behaviour of a State whose chief concern was her own safety, at a time when she could not take her safety for granted; of a State that had no overseas ambitions, and was herself conscious of no moral responsibilities outside herself. It is unjust to criticize Rome for that; it is a phase through which all States pass during their growth and development; and the fair question is whether within the limits of her development she behaved with moderation and a sense of responsibility. Her refusal to extend her territory proves both her moderation and also her city-state mentality, her patience with the Greeks, whose problems she did not understand, and whom she therefore came to despise for not behaving like Romans, was considerable. She tried hard to make a contented Greece and could not understand the reason for her failure; it was only after fifty years of sincere effort that her patience broke down.

Her policy towards more distant States followed the same pattern of guarding her security without involving herself in responsibility for the welfare of the States. Since her safety was only remotely involved at the periphery, her policy consisted in the maintenance of a balance of power between the important States, and a complete lack of interest otherwise. We need not examine the details of her interference and advice in the East; in her dealings with Pergamum and Egypt the checking of Syria's power was her main aim, and beyond the maintenance of a balance of power she did not aspire to go. It was a frontier policy, such as the emperors pursued with Armenia and Parthia, and the British in many parts of the world.

By her defeat of Carthage, Rome had become one of the powerful States of the Mediterranean world, but certainly not the most powerful; and, more important, was not conscious that she had entered the ranks of the powerful States. She might look upon her achievement with something of the awe with which the Athenians regarded Marathon; but she could not see that Zama had put her in a posture to stand as an equal beside the powerful Hellenistic monarchies. Situations may change in a day; but it often takes decades to discover the fact.

Rome was now in fact a powerful State, and with the passing of the years she grew more powerful in comparison with the other States. But there was no change in her mental outlook to correspond with her changed position. She was still, as she always had been, apprehensive of powers that might seem to present a threat to her safety; and this attitude of self-defensive apprehension characterizes her foreign policy throughout this period. Her mental outlook continued that of the city-state, whose sphere of responsibility was confined to its own interests, its self-preservation and the provision of what was necessary for that purpose. There is a great difference between a powerful State—which Rome was—and what I may call a "world-power"—which Rome was not—a difference not merely of relation to other States but of mental outlook and conception of moral responsibility. When a State has reached that point where she is incontestably the strongest power, with whom none singly within her sphere may hope to join issue, as Rome in Imperial times, England in the later nineteenth century, the U.S.A. today, I call such States "world-powers." In such circumstances the State may abandon its traditional attitude of self-defence and apprehension, and awaken to a sense of responsibility towards the weaker States who must look to her for help, or she may rejoice to have no further obstacle to the exploitation of her strength, which none can now prevent. This change from the outlook of a powerful State to that of a "world-power" may come as the result of a gradual realization of her new position, as it did with England, or as the result of violent convulsions within the State or the system of which that State is a part, as happened in Rome and the U.S.A. But there will necessarily be a political time-lag between the time at which all the material conditions of a "world-power" were satisfied and the realization of that fact by the State. There will be a period of which it will be possible in retrospect to say that the policy of the State was governed by considerations of self-defence, though there was nothing to fear, when she should more properly have been concerned with her responsibilities towards others. In 200 B.C. Rome was a powerful State; by 146 B.C. she was ready to be a "world-power," but did not realize it. That realization was frustrated for a century by the Gracchi, nor did it come until the Pax Augusta, which put an end to a century's civil discord.

We must, therefore, consider Rome's foreign policy from this point of view, from which alone we are justified in considering it; it is wrong to apply canons of criticism to her behaviour which are applicable to a State indisputably the strongest in her world, and aware of some at least of the attendant responsibilities. It is as a powerful State, with the organization and mentality of a city-state, that she must be criticized, and her success or failure, her consciousness of moral obligations must be measured by this standard.

We may take three incidents which illustrate the limitation—if it is proper to call limitation what is more truly lack of development—in Rome's outlook during these years, the destruction of Corinth, of Carthage, and her treatment of Rhodes.

At first sight the destruction of Corinth seems an act of wanton and irresponsible behaviour by a strong State towards a city that, however provoking, could never deserve such a fate. But Rome had not yet consciously calculated her strength in comparison with the rest of the world, and hence had not appreciated the implications of her superior strength; her reactions towards the outside world were the same as they had been at the beginning of the century. It was still axiomatic that Greece must be a Roman protectorate, even though, had she but thought, there was now no strong power to occupy it. She still felt no responsibility towards Greece, and still expected Greece to run her own affairs "freely," yet without causing trouble for Rome. When the Achaean League became—to Rome, incomprehensibly—thoroughly disgruntled and actually made war on Rome, patience snapped, the "independence" which the Greeks perversely refused to enjoy was taken from them, and Rome resigned herself to administering the country which stubbornly refused to run itself.

The sack of Corinth, a city rich in history and in the possession of artistic treasures, seemed to the ancient world a terrible thing. Yet to the Roman mind it was the punishment meted out by an angry victor as a warning; just as Carthage, Numantia, and Fregellae would suffer, and as Plataea and Thebes had suffered at the hands of the Greeks themselves in the days of their greatness. Rome behaved at this moment as a strong power that was governed by all the considerations that had shaped her policy for fifty years, and while the rest of the world could see Rome's overwhelming power and hence the needlessness of the act, Rome could not see herself as others saw her. Its effect on the contemporary world was great, because they feared what this mammoth might do next;

she might turn to ruthless conquest, which might engulf them. In fact, the history of the previous fifty years had shown, had they been in a position to see, that this would not be; it was one of her last preventive acts, a reflex action made at a time when it had become superfluous; hence both their disquiet and the needlessness for that disquiet.

The destruction of Carthage in the same year illustrates even more clearly this critical moment in Rome's political and moral development. The name of Carthage could arouse quite irrational fears in the breasts of the Romans; there were still alive a few who had lived through the Hannibalic War, and to all of them the story of the terrible fight, the defeats, the near-disaster was a source of fear, should it recur. They had consistently supported Massinissa against Carthage, the unknown against the known, and while none of Massinissa's actions roused their fear, anything that Carthage attempted provoked immediate retaliation. They could not see the situation in perspective; their thoughts and reactions were those of Rome the city-state, who must be on her guard to prevent the growth of any State able to threaten her security; and the very name of Carthage was too wrapped about with fearful memories to make reason and tolerance easy. Hence they behaved dishonourably, and were not content until they had removed their fear by razing the supposed threat and scattering its inhabitants.

Particularly instructive as an indication of the political theory and the psychology that lay behind it is the reason given by Scipio Nasica for allowing Carthage to continue: in order that there should be some State of whom Rome stood in awe. Here we see the enunciation of the political thought which had directed Rome's policy during these years, the ultimate position of the preventive, self-defensive atti-

tude. It is the proof that the Romans had not woken up to the responsibilities of a "world-power," that they were not yet aware that they were one. Scipio could see only that if Rome were wholly safe, if in fact she were to achieve what her foreign policy for fifty years had set out to achieve, then the Romans might start behaving irresponsibly, and her self-discipline might be corrupted. The attitude of Scipio Aemilianus, on the other hand, who approved its utter destruction, was the logical consequence of that policy; if her aim was to guard her security, then it was best guarded by destroying all possible opponents.

This was the critical moment in the story of Rome's growth to world dominion. It was symbolized by the unnecessary destruction of these two cities in pursuance of a policy which had directed her actions for generations, and had now become out of date. She had seemingly nothing more to do; she had attained her object; what, then, next? Well might the world wait expectantly to see the direction of her next step, for the world lay at Rome's mercy.

The consummation of their lifetime's policy left the minds of Rome's leaders temporarily without direction. There was a relaxation of tension, now that they had achieved their aim, before some fresh ideal was set before them, and that relaxation showed itself in many spheres; the protraction of the Spanish War, marked as it was by incompetence and dishonesty, by lack of discipline in the army, was one sign of it; now began that deterioration in standards of honesty and propriety which Polybius notes, and which we know from Lucilius to have been a source of concern to Scipio's circle. But such a temporary relaxation was natural, if unfortunate; the important point is that it was far from universal, and that the better men were worried by its manifestation. The solution could consist only in the creation of some ideal of policy to replace the one that had been achieved, and must take the form of some *ratio imperii*. Had their minds not been temporarily devoid of policy, it is unlikely that the Gracchi could have had so profound an effect.

The problem was great, far greater than most modern historians are prepared to concede; it was nothing less than the problem of emerging from the mentality and organization of a city-state to become the capital of an Empire, with a sense of moral responsibility not only to her own provinces but to the rest of the world. The days when Rome could think only of herself were past, and a complete reorientation was necessary for her new role; Stoic philosophers, seeing the problem from outside, might help, but only Romans could do it. Theirs was the problem to prepare for the future without destroying the past, and such reform can come only from within. Only a Roman could know how to change Rome's city-state institutions without uprooting society in the process.

Her changing relations and treatment of Rhodes illustrate a similar tendency in her policy during these years. Rhodes was a strong and important member of the Mediterranean community in 200 B.C., and for some years, while her policy led her to help Rome, she was rewarded, listened to with respect and held in high esteem. But Rhodes, able to observe impartially the gradually changing Mediterranean situation, began to realize that Rome in the process of protecting herself from her supposed enemies was herself becoming very powerful and a source of anxiety to other States. Rhodes realized that she must depend for a continuance of her position and influence on a balance of power between the great States, of which she numbered Rome one, and she was consequently not wholly favourable to Rome

in the third Macedonian War. She perceived that the complete defeat of Perseus would leave Rome unpleasantly the strongest State, against which it would be idle for Rhodes to match her strength. Her sympathies, therefore, like those of several others, were with Perseus. The smaller Mediterranean States were beginning to be uneasy at Rome's growth, and to feel that a strong Macedon was a guarantee against Roman tyranny.

Rome won and Rhodes suffered. Saved from war by the sympathetic and forthright speaking of Cato, she was punished and in the event reduced to economic impotence. We should, however, note that Rhodes' reason for not wanting the complete defeat of Perseus was similar to Scipio Nasica's argument against the destruction of Carthage, and it reflects the general attitude of most contemporaries towards a powerful State. Experience had taught them that powerful states tended to embark on wars of conquest, and the best protection was a second powerful State; if Rome had not yet risen to the consciousness of a moral responsibility towards others, nor had anyone else; it was only when Rome stood preeminent that the Greek world became seriously concerned about the responsibilities involved in such a position, and then primarily because they were worried for themselves.

But if Rome was still groping towards a broader vision, she was not a mere freebooter. Though Rhodes was punished, it was not Rome who gained by it; the free port of Delos did not increase Rome's income. The suggestion that Rome should make war on Rhodes illustrates again Rome's state of mind, a state wherein one cannot see that one's cause is not necessarily universally approved, and that other people may have different views. A more mature and cynical diplomacy knows the hollowness of so many pretensions, and may smile but keep temper if thwarted or opposed. But Rome was seeking nothing but security, and therefore did not appreciate the reasons for opposition to a policy which aimed at hurting no one. Further, it may help to caution us from regarding the destruction of Corinth as a sign of degenerating morality; had Rhodes been as great a nuisance at this moment as Greece became by 146 B.C., she would probably have suffered a similar fate.

The slim volume *Roman Imperialism in the Late Republic* by E. BADIAN is based upon a set of lectures delivered at the University of South Africa in 1965. The occasion enabled Badian to deliver some general considerations on the nature of Roman imperialism. Here he outlines the differences between Roman policy in the western provinces and that in the east. The differences were dictated by the types of people with whom Rome had to deal, and were not due to a change in purpose or motivation. In Badian's view, foreign policy sprang from domestic attitudes. Rome's treatment of foreign states was an outgrowth of her own internal system of patronage and clientage.*

E. Badian

Patron-State and Client-State

Imperialism in some sense is as old as the human race, or at least as its social organisation. The extension of power by one's own group over others is only a special case of the victory of one's own side over others: in human terms, it does not call for an explanation. The naive joy in this that we find in Victorian imperialists or (for that matter) in a modern football crowd is as obvious in Cicero, with his numerous proud references to the glory and the victories of the Roman People—which are almost the only serious ideas he developed in public about the theory and practice of politics beyond his own community!

What does call for an explanation, when it appears in history, is that relatively high

level of sophistication that *rejects* opportunities for the extension of power. As in the curbing of private ambition, either or both of two motives may lead to this: we may call them considerations of expediency or morality—in Roman terms, the *utile* and the *honestum*. The individual may realise that the pursuit of his ambition may be bad for his health or happiness; or he may come to question the principle of competition and the pursuit of power and distinction as a motive force. Similarly the community. We are not going to be concerned with the *merits* of this: in the first case one may speak of prudence or pusillanimity, in the second of saintliness or neurotic decadence. Our point is only that both these mo-

*Reprinted from E. Badian: *Roman Imperialism in the Late Republic.* Copyright © Basil Blackwell, 1968. Used by permission of Cornell University Press and Basil Blackwell and Mott, Ltd. Pp. 1-15. Footnotes omitted.

tives, in their different ways, are signs of sophistication, overcoming the deep-seated urge for domination and power.

Policy at Rome, as we all now know, was in practice determined by a governing oligarchy, which reached its zenith in the second century B.C. Its attitude to our question was a highly complex one. It had long outgrown the most primitive stage: indeed, as Mommsen recognised long ago, most of the second century is characterised by a highly sophisticated policy of avoiding annexation. In the West, Carthage had been left standing in 201, and its chances of future prosperity little diminished. In the East, Philip V of Macedon had been defeated by 196 and a decision of principle had to be taken. Titus Quinctius Flamininus, combining the methods of Roman with the lessons of Greek history (which he will certainly have known), convinced the Senate that Rome must appear as the liberator of the Greeks while pursuing what was in effect her traditional policy. So the "freedom of the Greeks" was proclaimed in a theatrical scene at the Isthmian Games of 196; and though there was strong pressure among cautious senators for the military occupation of at least some key fortresses in Greece, Flamininus in the end overcame it and, after the war with Nabis of Sparta, withdrew all the Roman troops. The decision had been taken and was not reversed, despite the opposition of the great Scipio. Indeed, against the threat of advance by Antiochus III, Rome (under Flamininus' direction) intensified its propaganda efforts to appear as the champion of Greek freedom against enslavement to kings and oppression. Once Antiochus had been defeated, this line proved unprofitable and was abandoned: in their cold-blooded attitude over this, the Romans showed, to all who would observe, their contempt of foreign opinion when it

no longer mattered. To leave all the Greeks free would have led to anarchy, while Rome now wanted order. But the principle of non-annexation was preserved—indeed, the very desire for order shows its strength. Rome wanted to be sure she would not have to intervene again. Eumenes of Pergamum and (to a lesser extent) the Republic of Rhodes received large increases of territory and became the protagonists of the Roman order in Asia. In Europe, Macedon was left intact, though not allowed to expand in Greece; and the Greeks continued without supervision. It is clear that the Senate hoped they would be able to run their own affairs, taking its advice, as loyal clients, when it was asked for or offered.

Indeed, this did not work out as planned: during the next generation, as one party after another kept appealing to Rome, and the clients ignored advice frequently given but never backed by force, the Senate—against its will, clearly—was drawn more and more into perpetual intervention, both to keep order and to restore its fading prestige. Yet the fact is that down to the war with Perseus, and again after it, no Roman governor or soldier was stationed east of the Adriatic, despite the astonishing successes that Roman arms had won as far to the east as Mount Taurus, and the equally astonishing failure to have Roman wishes in Greece consistently carried out.

When Macedon became more powerful and began to intrigue among the Greek states, the Senate—rightly or wrongly—came to the conclusion that another war would have to be fought. Questionable diplomacy was used; yet in the end there was again no annexation. The Aegean world after the battle of Pydna looked a very different place from what it had been before. The kingdom of Macedon was broken up into its four traditional constituent districts, which were made into separate "free" states. A thousand Achaeans, among them Polybius, were deported to Italy, and no doubt numbers of Greeks from other states. Rhodes was left humbled and its naval power broken. Pergamum had fallen into disfavour and was thrown open to attacks by hostile neighbours. Roman interference in Asia as in Europe had become open and undisguised, leaving no strong power anywhere to keep order as before. Yet it was still true that not a single Roman governor or soldier stood east of the Adriatic. Methods had changed; but the principles had remained, and indeed become even more obvious. The overriding aim, as before, was to avoid annexation (which, in terms of power, could easily have been imposed). The first method tried had been to leave one or two strong powers to keep order: they had become too strong and were thus felt to be dangerous to Rome. Now the only alternative that might achieve the aim was tried: weakness and fragmentation, with constant inspection—even at the risk of anarchy. But the assumption of direct responsibility was not even considered. Rome might still claim that her purpose was merely to ensure peace and prevent threats to her safety.

Yet, clearly, this is only half the picture. Nothing could be further from the truth than to suppose that the Roman oligarchy felt a moral repugnance towards aggression and domination or believed in the co-existence of equal and fully sovereign states. Indeed, to the last century of the Republic, the censors by custom had to pray to the gods for an increase in the possessions of the Roman people. Whether or not individual Roman nobles ever seriously believed that the threat of foreign powers was necessary to maintain the soundness of the Roman body politic—a view that, even if P. Scipio Nasica did in fact express it in

opposition to the elder Cato, was blown up into a political principle only *ex post facto*—there is no doubt that such a view never provided a basis of action for the Roman state as such. Roman policy in Greece early in the century, and in the Aegean area as a whole after 167, shows a mixture of petulance and arrogance that, despite its failure to obtain obedience to Roman wishes in detail, was only too successful in perpetuating intrigue and tension and preventing the emergence of any strong power. Non-annexation, in fact, never meant non-intervention.

Roman imperialism can therefore still be said to have existed in the East; but it was not of the annexationist kind: it was of what we may call the "hegemonial" kind. On the barbarian fringe of the Empire, on the other hand, war never stopped. In Spain, Liguria or Sardinia no settled frontier ever existed. For decades slow conquest, interrupted by many setbacks, gradually expanded the occupied and pacified zone. We hear few details of all these operations, except in a handful of spectacular cases: they were taken for granted. Hence, though the facts are obvious enough, their significance is easily overlooked. Yet both the similarities and the differences between Roman policy towards civilised and towards barbarian states are striking. We must come back to them later.

It might be thought that the failure to admit the independent existence of other powers and their right to run their affairs without intervention from outside was due to the spirit of the age—a tradition from which Rome merely failed to escape. Yet this does not seem to have been so. Whatever had been the case in Classical Greece (and it was perhaps not so very different from what followed), a concert of Hellenistic powers had existed for a century when Rome so violently intruded upon it. The principal Hellenistic states, while often engaged in wars over contested territories and in intrigues to undermine one another's influence, seem, after two generations of anarchy following the death of Alexander the Great, to have recognized an equilibrium on the general maintenance of which the independent existence of each of them was based. The Ptolemies, the Seleucids, the Antigonids, as well as smaller powers like Pergamum, Bithynia or even the Aetolian and Achaean Leagues—they all had their part to play, and the disappearance of any of them would have led to a major catastrophe. Very probably, this was merely a recognition of the limitations of the various Hellenistic powers—it was based purely on expediency. But it was nevertheless effective in recreating a relatively stable world in the third century. The Hellenistic world, like that of modern Europe for centuries before the Great War, was one based on a balance that, as each power knew, had to be preserved at least in essentials.

Roman policy, from almost as far back as we can trace it, was different. Of course, for a long time Rome had to recognise the equality of some other powers: thus in the early treaties with Carthage recorded by Polybius. Indeed, before 218 B.C. she could hardly have *denied* equality to Carthage or to the great powers of the East. But right from the start there was the determination to dominate whatever was within reach and to build up strength to extend that reach. Equality was conceded only beyond the range of effective power, and every attempt was made to build up power where it had shown itself deficient. It is clear that the Romans always ended up by heavily outnumbering their rivals. By the middle of the fourth century, hegemony had been claimed over Latium, while the Samnites were an equal enemy—or (as in the Latin War) ally. By the time of the war with Pyrrhus, the whole of Italy was claimed as

a hegemonial sphere, and victory justified the claim. By the end of the twenties it had been extended to the adjacent islands and to territories across the Ionian and Adriatic Seas. Within the areas thus staked out, independent states were, after a fashion, permitted and even encouraged to exist: like the many Italian states with their different treaties, or the kingdoms and free cities of Sicily and Illyria. But, whatever the exact status of those communities, in what Rome regarded as essential—their foreign policy—they were effectively under Roman control. The state of affairs that we found so characteristic of Roman policy in the second century, and so surprising in its Hellenistic context, had always been the same, as far as Rome was concerned.

On two occasions, as Rome came into contact with the Hellenistic concert of powers, it looked for a moment as though she might adopt its standards and fit her different traditions and organisation into that Greek world that so obviously attracted her leading citizens. First, in the Peace of Phoenice (205 B.C.) it seems a genuine attempt was made to secure co-existence on equal terms with Philip V by leaving an insulating layer of buffer states between the two powers. Had this succeeded, Rome might have stopped there (as far as the East was concerned)—at least long enough to become pervaded with the new concept of a polity and a balance of states. But Philip, over-confident, began to interfere with the buffer states in Illyria while at the same time extending his power in the East. The causes of the Second Macedonian War have been interminably discussed. It is clear that it was in fact due to Roman suspicion of Philip's successes and ambitious policies on various fronts, seen against the background of his "stab in the back" in the Hannibalic War. But I have elsewhere tried to bring out—certainly not as the only, but as a very obvious cause—what is indeed obvious in Livy's account: the breakdown of the Illyrian settlement, at the only point where the two powers met and directly clashed. An attempt had been made at Phoenice to secure peace; but Philip had made it impossible. The result was the war that established Roman hegemony over Greece and Macedonia.

The next turning-point came when, at a secret conference in Rome, Titus Quinctius Flamininus faced the envoys of Antiochus III and made them an offer in terms of cold-blooded geopolitics, contrasting with his carefully developed public propaganda position: if the King kept out of Europe, Rome would keep out of Asia. There is no reason to doubt that he—and the Senate—meant it. But again an Eastern king, over-confident in his strength, refused to settle. The result was the war that ended at Magnesia and Apamea. Henceforth—at least until the Parthians were seen to be dangerous—there were no equals left. Rome never again behaved as if there were.

The puzzling contradiction in Roman policy—open aggression and expansionism against barbarians; hegemonial imperialism with careful avoidance of annexation towards cultural equals or superiors—this peculiar adaptation of the urge for domination that underlies them both cannot, of course, be exhaustively explained, any more than any other phenomenon of any importance and complexity in historical enquiry. But there are some clues we should follow. First, it became clear to the Roman governing class at an early stage that large increases of territory could not easily be administered within the existing city-state constitution. Rather than change the latter—which was inconceivable, though minor adaptations (such as the promagistracy) were freely tried—annexation was, on the whole, soon abandoned for

subordination by treaty. With power expanding beyond Italy, even this became too burdensome, since it imposed definite and often inconvenient commitments on Rome. Hence the further step towards the "free" ally, city or king, controlled without a treaty. It must be confessed that under the Roman Republic no real system of administering overseas territories was ever evolved: those that were annexed (like most of Sicily and Sardinia) were merely the allotted spheres of action (*prouinciae*) of a military commandant (at first normally a praetor) who, right until the end of the Republic, governed under what was not far removed from a permanent (though slightly regularised) state of siege. But that is another story. Meanwhile we must notice that, down to the middle of the second century, all but one of the provinces remained active theatres of war—rich in triumphs, but costly to the state. Sicily was probably the only one that regularly realised a surplus for the Treasury. The rest were a constant drain in money—and, worse still, in manpower. Rome and Italy could hardly cope with the demand. Small wonder, therefore, that the Senate was slow to start major wars when it could be avoided—and certainly not for the sake of annexation, which, more often than not, proved merely a prelude to a future of minor wars.

Moreover, early in the second century the Scipios had given a terrible warning to the majority of their peers. Adopting names to represent the *orbis terrarum* they claimed to have conquered (Africanus, Asiaticus, Hispallus), they had threatened—not indeed a military tyranny, as some later Romans thought and some modern authors still hanker after saying: for this was quite inconceivable at the time—no, they had threatened to acquire an overpowering prestige that might make the egalitarian working of oligarchic government practically impossible. The Scipios had gone down to defeat; but their example remained, and the lesson was learnt: great overseas commands were carefully avoided.

There is another point to consider. We shall have to say some harsh things about the Senate in due course; but let us give praise where it is due. It is all the more necessary to stress that it looks as if concern over standards of magistrates' behaviour in the provinces was another powerful influence in discouraging annexation and its consequence, direct administration. There was trouble quite early: in 171 B.C. major complaints came from Spain about the actions of governors there. Not much was done: some of the men were well connected. The Roman oligarchy, like other oligarchies, was reluctant to punish its members for the sake of its subjects. There was more trouble in the fifties. The excessive powers enjoyed by the holders of *imperium* were bound to corrupt. What is more, they led to an excess of pride and individualism—for which Hellenistic cultural influence often gets the blame. This would make men stand out against the Senate. Livy offers many examples of disobedient magistrates at the height of the Senate's power. Some succeeded in their designs or at least went unpunished: it was never easy to exercise effective control. Nor could the mercurial popular assembly be relied on for a responsible judgment. There can be no doubt that these considerations weighed heavily with the Senate as a whole in its set policy of minimising overseas commitments.

It is significant that the first serious attempt to deal with the problem of misbehaviour in the provinces comes in 149. In that year L. Calpurnius Piso, the virtuous tribune surnamed Frugi, passed the first law that was to enable oppressed allies at least to get back what they had lost. A permanent *quaestio repetundarum* was set up, to take the place of the all too frequent *ad hoc* commissions of the Senate for this purpose. There were no severe penalties (if there were any), for the time being. Rightly, one is inclined to think. It became only too clear in the later Republic that severe extortion laws merely made senatorial juries (and not only them) more unwilling to convict, and more amenable to the sort of appeal for sympathy for a Roman senator against wretched foreigners at which Cicero (when it suited him) was such a master. Piso's law seems to have provided merely for restitution. Obviously, it was really meant to work. Now, what is most significant about it, perhaps, is its date. For in 149 the war against Carthage had started, and it is clear that the Senate was beginning to realise that this time there was no solution short of annexation. In the same year, the praetor P. Iuventius Thalna was defeated by the pretender Andriscus, who had united Macedonia (which the Romans had divided up) against the settlement of 167. Again, it is reasonable to think that the Senate knew that another experiment in non-annexation had failed. It is therefore interesting—and to the credit of the Fathers—that precisely in that year, with large-scale further annexation imminent and inevitable, they made an honest attempt to protect their subjects against the worst effects of misbehaviour on the part of magistrates. The Senate as a whole—as it was to show as late as 95, when it sent Q. Mucius Scaevola to Asia, not to mention 72, when the consuls proposed a decree at least trying to curb Verres—the Senate, in 149 as at other times, took its responsibilities seriously. This gives us the right of positing such considerations as among the motives for the avoidance of annexation.

As far as the Hellenistic East is concerned, an important political consideration may be added. Early in the second century T. Flamininus discovered what monarchs had known for generations: the power of Greek public opinion. Gradually he converted the Senate to his views. Political hegemony in the East traditionally depended on at least a modicum of co-operation. Hence relations with at least some of the kings, leagues and cities were—most of the time—carefully watched, to secure and retain the approval of those who mattered. It was a civilised and interconnected world, where—as in ours—political actions at once received vast publicity. This had to be considered; and the war against Perseus, with its vicissitudes, made it even clearer. Very different was the situation on the barbarian "frontier": there no one (except perhaps a man's *inimici,* for their private profit) greatly cared what was done to a Ligurian or Iberian tribe. The record of Roman war and policy in Spain—as, in particular, A. Schulten insisted—is one of cruelty and treachery almost unparalleled in Roman history. Yet not a single commander came to serious harm as a result: not the perfidious mass murderer Ser. Sulpicius Galba, whom Cato tried to attack, but who survived to be an honoured master of Roman oratory; nor C. Hostilius Mancinus, who made a treaty with the Numantines which he probably knew the Senate would dishonour: handed over to them, naked and bound, in expiation, he found (as he had no doubt expected) that the barbarians were far too humane to punish him; whereupon he returned to Rome, was allowed to resume his citizenship and soon rose to be praetor again.

Thus a double standard of behaviour developed. In the East, a hegemonial policy was pursued in a cautious and, on the whole, fairly civilised way, at least without violence and open treachery and certainly (as long as it proved possible) without direct control and major wars. But against the barbarians, where publicity need not be feared and where, incidentally, the gradual advancing of the frontier did not, on the whole, lead to any major new commitment at any one time, so that the whole process would not easily become obvious— there policy was openly brutal and aggressive, and triumph-hunting an accepted technique.

Of course, in this distinction in what was permitted towards barbarians and what towards Hellenes (i.e., at this time, civilised states) the Romans were fitting themselves into a Greek tradition that went back a long time. In Greece it can be demonstrated as early as the fifth century; while in Roman policy, as late as the First Macedonian War, there is no sign of such a distinction. And so, even if tales of Roman behaviour in the West did filter through to Greek cities, the Romans had nothing to fear: it is doubtful whether anyone other than a few philosophers cared. As for the principle of fetial law, that no war was acceptable to the gods unless it was waged in defence of one's own country or one's allies—whether this applied to native tribes is not quite certain; though in theory it probably did. But, as is well known, the law was by now a mere ritual, robbed of all real content. The Romans had quite early developed a standard technique for evading ritual pollution: to make an alliance with a state exposed to certain attack and to defend it when the attack came. A variant of this can be observed, with a further loosening of the legal element, in the ultimatum that preceded the Second Macedonian War. But in the second century, though it is possible that the ritual was still performed—perhaps even as late as the Jugurthine War—none of our sources pays the slightest attention to it, and as far as its motive power in policy is concerned, we must clearly follow them and ignore it.

As we have seen, the double standard of behaviour yet went back to a single basic attitude. Both the bellicose annexationism and the hegemonial policy spring from deeply rooted features of Roman life. It is these that we must now briefly consider. The values of Roman aristocratic life were those characteristic of that form of society. High birth and merit (*genus* and *uirtus*) were chiefy admired. The former— descent from distinguished ancestors—was taken to be a *prima facie* guarantee of the latter, imposing both a standard and a challenge. The latter (*uirtus*) was the real touchstone of achievement and the only claim that could be advanced by the "new man," who lacked the guarantee of high birth. The aristocratic poet Lucilius, at the end of a long passage full of high-sounding Greek sentiment, defined it in a few simple words: "commoda patriai prima putare." *Virtus* as an aristocratic Roman concept has been much discussed. It has even been suggested that originally the term meant a primitive magic power, a kind of *mana,* which naturally inhered in leading men. This meaning, if it ever existed, was, of course, much changed by the second century, particularly as Greek philosophy began to affect Roman education. But the quality was always most fully embodied in the commander and statesman: it was very much a *public* virtue, and one of the ruling class—at least, as seen by that class. Its chief example was, as we have seen, the man who, having the deeds of great ancestors as a model, administered the state in war and peace to its greatest advantage. The Roman aristocracy was always conscious of its destiny.

What really counted, by the second century, is perhaps best seen in the famous epitaphs of the Scipios. It was—if one ignored a few Greek ideas that, as Lucilius' poetic discussion shows, did not count for so very much in the practical test—descent, offices and military success.

L. Cornelius Scipio Barbatus (consul 298 B.C.) boasts that his *forma uirtutei parisuma fuit* (thus making his bow to Greek admiration for beauty, but clearly distinguishing it from Roman *uirtus*). He goes on, in a very Roman way, to give proof of his *uirtus,* which is clearly what really counts: he gives his offices (*consol censor aidilis quei fuit apud uos*) and finally his great deeds in war (*Taurasia Cisaunia Samnio cepit, subigit omne Loucanam opsidesque abdoucit*). Barbatus' son (consul 259) claims to be, by common consent, the best man of all Romans (*duonoro optumo fuise uiro*). Again he illustrates this with his offices (consulate, censorship, aedileship) and his victories (*hec cepet Corsica Aleriaque urbe*); finally he cites his *pietas* in dedicating a temple, thus bringing in a religious element that is surprisingly rare elsewhere. But most eloquent, perhaps, is the epitaph of a young L. Scipio, a son of the great Asiaticus, who died as a quaestorian of 33 and thus had no chance of demonstrating his *uirtus* in command and high administration. He proudly claims: *pater regem Antioco subegit.* At least he could be proud of his father's *uirtus.*

Military success and the holding of office: these are the chief claims to *uirtus.* Within the aristocracy, as we all know, Roman politics, especially in the second century B.C. was a constant struggle for prestige (*dignitas*), pursued with single-minded ambition. It was a highly competitive society. But this prestige, as we have seen even from contemporary evidence, found its chief support in the holding of office and in military success. This requisite glory had to be gathered somewhere. And since in the second century major wars, and wars against civilised states, were (as we have found) on the whole against public policy, it had to be gathered on the barbarian frontier. There it would not commit the State (at least at any one time) to more than it could undertake; it would not endanger Rome's public reputation; and the successes gained would not be so overpowering as to arouse fear and *inuidia* among a man's peers. Triumphs were essential to the Roman way of life and politics; and it is not surprising that triumph-hunting against barbarians became a recognised pursuit—a matter of political life or death to many a Roman noble. Even in the first century, a man's refusal to indulge in it could be used by an enemy to attack his character and damn his reputation.

The other aspect—the hegemonial policy—goes back to an equally characteristic tradition of the Roman aristocracy: that of patronage. From the very start of Roman history, powerful men had had free "clients" attached to their persons and families. These men, though legally free, were by custom—and by the facts of power—obliged to obey and serve their patron in return for his protection. In a wider sense of the word, every *beneficium* created a relation of clientship, obliging the recipient to be prepared to render *officia*. Naturally, the ability to confer *beneficia* was, on the whole, also an aristocratic privilege; so that, in addition to their direct dependants, upper-class individuals and families were surrounded by a circle of others whom they had placed under an obligation and who were expected to repay them on demand.

It was in this way, to a large extent, that the oligarchy maintained its power for so long in the Roman state; and it was in this way that rivals fought each other for office and prestige: indeed, the latter was, to a certain extent, visibly measured by the number of clients a man could muster. Inevitably, these relationships spread beyond the city of Rome and its territory, as Rome came into contact with places and people more and more remote—first to Italy, then to the provinces, "free" cities and even neighbouring monarchs. Both collectively and as individuals, men abroad owed *officia* to the Roman aristocrats who had conferred *beneficia* on them, e.g. by governing them, by sparing them after victory, by looking after their interests in Rome. It was a natural consequence that Roman aristocrats, accustomed to seeing personal relationships, both within the community and outside, in these terms of moral relationships and duties based (ultimately) on the facts of power, should transfer this attitude to their political thinking: that Rome in fact, should appear as the patron city, claiming the *officia* both of actual allies and subjects and of "free" kings and cities with which she had come into contact. These attitudes were woven into the Roman noble's life. Of course, it was the oligarchy, acting through the Senate, that represented Rome—the patronal power—in its relations with those clients, thus reinforcing the bonds of individual clientship that personally united many of them to great Roman houses. It was clear that the whole world owed *officia* to the great power acting through the men who governed it. As Roman power increased, it became impossible, for those brought up under this system, to see any relationship between Romans and foreigners, between Rome and foreign states, in other terms than these; and this explains what often—by our standards—seems arrogance and even naiveté in Roman behaviour. The obedience of the weak to the strong was, to the Roman aristocrat, nothing less than an eternal moral law.

The effects of Roman expansion were far-reaching. The results were evident not only abroad but, more strikingly, at home. A new commercial and business class rose to challenge the traditional authority of the landowning aristocracy. The agricultural pattern was shattered by the development of large estates for profit, the influx of slaves, and the growth of an urban proletariat. The simple social and military structure of the early Republic yielded to a more complex and more volatile situation. A. H. McDONALD (b. 1908), fellow of Clare College, Cambridge, author of numerous articles on Republican history, and editor of the Oxford text of Livy, here traces some of these developments as the consequence of Roman imperialism.*

A. H. McDonald

Economic and Social Consequences of Imperialism

Rome's expansion in Italy did not disturb the setting of aristocratic leadership. The nobles remained good landowners and responsible politicians. They organized their connexions with other families so as to secure their position, through suitable marriages and, where necessary, by the adoption of sons, and play their part in public life from one generation to another; their education and training were directed to these ends. Such is the conduct of aristocratic government in normal times. Where urgent problems arose, however, they used independent judgement, settling their differences of opinion, in order to achieve a common policy, and there was scope for outstanding individuals to make their mark, especially in military commands. While the family ambitions for civic dignity coloured the background of politics, Rome would not have won an empire if her leaders had failed in their patriotic duty. Above all, the pressure of external danger enforced the unity of the people. The Romans later admitted that the effects of victory changed their standards of public morality.

During the third century B.C. we may note the growth of the administrative system through which the nobles exercised their leadership. They encouraged and regulated the progress of technical skill in engineering, roadmaking, town planning and public building, developments that would increase their strength. Rome now spoke for Italy, and the Greek states recog-

*From A. H. McDonald in *The Romans,* edited by J. P. V. D. Balsdon (London: C. A. Watts & Co. Ltd., 1965), pp. 10-19, 22-26. Footnotes omitted.

nized her importance in the Western world; in 273 B.C. Ptolemaic Egypt opened political relations. About 269 Rome struck her first silver and established a bimetallic currency of silver and bronze, initially to meet the conditions in southern Italy. The First Punic War took the legions to Sicily and forced Rome into naval activity: one does not build, man, equip and supply fleets without an efficient shore establishment. In the Second Punic War Hannibal set a major problem of handling manpower and supporting military operations: there were Roman armies in Spain, Sicily and Greece, as well as in Italy—not to forget the ships at sea—before the war was over. Then the campaigns in Spain, Cisalpine Gaul and the east added to Rome's experience in the technique of war and confirmed her militaristic methods. . . .

Constitutionally an advisory body, the Senate had assumed many of the functions of direct administration, in terms of policy, appointments, and finance. It became a war council, using the experience of its members and devoting its full attention to the conduct of affairs, where a popular assembly was incapable of acting expeditiously or with successful judgement. Within the Senate the nobles made an inner circle: their influence dominated the Senate's deliberations, while their strongest men handled the practical affairs of state. How far would their judgement and good faith stand the test of imperial responsibility?

The new features of Roman life after the Mediterranean expansion are well known. It is usual to list them: the influx of wealth and investment in land, the importation of overseas grain, the supply of cheap slave labour, thus the spread of *latifundia* as estates supplying the cities, and the decline of the peasantry; the rise of a commercial and industrial class along with an urban proletariat; all of which led to the corrup-

tion of public life, weakness in the military system, and social unrest, leading to a revolutionary situation. The list is correct enough: the Romans themselves drew it up and emphasized the part of luxury in lowering the standards of traditional morality. But it is not enough to generalize in this way about seventy years of fundamental economic and social change such as most developing countries have had to experience. We have sufficient evidence from Polybius and Livy to attempt a closer analysis of the trends in Rome and Italy as well as the effect of Roman policy upon the Mediterranean.

The Second Punic War had displaced large numbers of the Italian population, especially in the south, and brought about strategic changes of economic activity, which strengthened the urban life of central Italy. Rome's military levies kept the young men on service, while the growth of war industries brought others into the cities; footloose veterans were as likely to take urban work as return to farming. Rome itself was the chief centre of production, and the Etruscan cities contributed to the supply of military equipment; after Hannibal's withdrawal Campania made an economic recovery. Overseas campaigning throughout the Mediterranean continued the demand for army material. We have to appreciate the general effect of this development; for the basic industries promoted the growth of the other trades and business occupations that support city life, and the increasing urban population provided a larger market for varied agricultural produce. Rome, for example, had to undertake more building and improve the city's water supply; the main trades required metals, leather, and wool; the workmen and their families needed grain, oil, and wine, which had to come cheaply and conveniently. The city had already begun to import grain in bulk, largely from

icily; this would expand the port of Ostia
nd its shipping. The other food supplies
ould be provided locally, if agriculture
dapted itself to the market needs. Such
roduction, however, was not the work of
easant farming but of specialized agricul-
ure with resources of capital, whether it
stablished olive groves and vineyeards or
eveloped the pastoral side. This kind of
rming, long practised in Etruria and
outhern Italy, was now encouraged by the
rban growth of Latium and Campania.
'he influx of wealth and slave labour had
et to take economic effect; but we can
lready discern the economic pattern
·hich would soon allow the profitable in-
estment of Roman capital in land.

Meanwhile the city of Rome had be-
ome a focus of commercial activity. In
93 B.C., since Roman money-lenders were
sing Latin agents in order to escape the
oman restriction on rates of interest,
ansactions of this kind were brought un-
er Roman law. At the same time Latins
ere moving into the city, where they
ould find work and acquire citizenship by
sidence, and the Latin states had diffi-
lty in raising their quota of troops. In
93 B.C. the consul agreed to take a pro-
ortion of the eligible men; but in 187, as
e drift went on, Rome agreed with the
atin authorities to repatriate Latins who
d migrated since 204. The implications
˙ this situation seem clear enough: that is,
cial conditions in Latium were changing
d the treaty relations were obsolete,
hile both the Roman and the Latin lead-
s hoped to save the old order. In Campa-
a the Capuans, who had lost their citizen-
ip after joining Hannibal, were re-en-
lled at Rome, as a step towards citizen-
ip again, while three municipalities with
ivate Roman rights were granted the full
ghts of citizenship; soon the ancient
reek foundation of Cumae would use Lat-
as its official language. All this is evidence

for the closer social organization of
central Italy.

In southern Italy, where Hannibal's occupation and the Roman measures of recovery had disrupted the life of the country, it was left to local enterprise to restore
normal conditions. Here the Greek cities,
as they recovered, and the rural gentry
took the lead. When Rome let out her
public land again, the local landowners
leased it in order to farm it in conjunction
with their own estates, and they increased
their stock in the confidence that they
would have security of tenure. Their
grandsons would be horrified when the
Gracchan agrarian legislation took this
land from them.

In 187 B.C. the legions were back from
the east and the long period of imperial
expansion came to an end. There was still
need for military levies in operations that
established two provinces in Spain and
brought Cisalpine Gaul and Sardinia under control, and the legions would return
to Greece to destroy the ancient kingdom
of Macedon in 171–168 B.C. Even then armies were kept standing in provinces, especially in Spain, where their presence
would maintain order; the old militia system was not well suited to these overseas
demands. Above all, the changes in Rome
and Italy raised difficulties which the Roman leaders, aristocratic in spirit and militaristic in their experience, were slow to
understand, and their position enabled
them to resist the pressure of circumstances. The Italian nobles, too, preferred
a policy that would not threaten their local
influence—as long as Rome did not sacri-
fice their interests.

The Roman government repaid its citizens twenty-five and a half imposts of taxation which the wars had made necessary,
and it was able to embark upon a programme of public expenditure, especially
in the crowded cities. We learn of an

abundance of money on the Roman market in 186 B.C.; it would include the profit which generals, officers and soldiers had made in the eastern wars. From this time it is fair to assume that capital played a decisive part in expanding the Roman economy along the lines it was already following. The contractors enlarged their operations; the senatorial class invested their wealth in the only secure field of business available to them, viz., in agriculture, but it was the new agriculture that served the needs of the urban markets. Soon the supply of slave labour became relevant; for the enslavement of 80,000 Sardinians in 176 and the enslavement of 150,000 Epirotes in 167 B.C.—even if they did not all come to Italy—exercised a strong economic effect, especially on the growth of large country estates.

Meanwhile the soldiers who had fought in Greece, under conditions that encouraged plunder and licence, brought back habits of Eastern luxury, more often than not to the cities, and the Roman moralists from Cato onwards would trace the decline of Roman conduct from this period. But we shall look rather to the state of Italy itself, influenced by the shift of population and the spread of Greek culture from the south. In 186 B.C. the Senate believed that the worship of Dionysus, with its orgiastic rites, had become a threat to public morality, and it decided to regulate the practice of the cult throughout Italy. Livy describes the harsh measures of repression and his account is confirmed by a copy of the decree which the consuls transmitted to the Italian allies, advising them how to act in their own locality. The Roman policy had portentous features. The Senate, in effect, was determined to control social behaviour, but it could only do so by treating misbehaviour as politically subversive, that is, as a "conspiracy" against the State; then the consuls could

take emergency measures, almost in term of martial law. Only on this basis, too could the Senate at all properly issue strong instruction to the allied authoritie But was the principle itself a proper one The definition of what constituted "con spiracy" and "emergency" had hithert covered conditions that posed a direc threat of violence to the State. How coul this include the excesses of a degenerat cult? Only by extending the definition of "subversion" far beyond its original scope for the Dionysiac devotees were hardly ca pable of overthrowing Rome. There is n more dangerous weapon in the hands of any government than the power to inten sify police action by arbitrary reinterpreta tion of the law; this is how dictatorship make a first parade of legality. Sixty yea later the Senate would turn this weapo against its Gracchan opponents: we hav here the germ of the "ultimate decree, the decree for "the defence of the State, which brought the element of force int the internal politics of Rome. For the mo ment the Senate aimed merely at using i authority to overcome the obstacles of earl er practice in Rome and Italy in order t meet the new circumstances. . . .

The Third Macedonian War (171–16 B.C.) brought the underlying discontents t the surface. Though the Senate was dete mined to crush Macedon, the army wa less ready to endure what turned out to b a tedious course of campaigning. Genera oppressed their Greek allies, soldiers san into slackness and insubordination, an when Rome called on her most ex perienced general, Aemilius Paullus, h had first to silence criticism at home an then restore discipline in the field befor he was able to win the war. The Sena made a brutal and unsatisfactory settl ment when it divided the Macedonia kingdom into four helpless republics an undermined the power of its allies Perga mum and Rhodes, whose influence was necessary to the life of the Aegean world. This was the policy of men who had lost the foresight of their fathers, sacrificing the element of goodwill that had served even the most strategic calculations in the past. At home the business (equestrian) class gained popular support against the censors of 169–168, such distinguished men as Sempronius Gracchus and C. Claudius Pulcher. Victory and the profits of war gave relief and the nobles felt secure again, but the balance of Roman affairs, under less pressure than Rome had borne a generation earlier, had betrayed its instability. And in 167 B.C. the Epirote slaves came on the market.

Among his many works Cato wrote a small book *On Agriculture,* and he was not a man to write to no purpose. He describes how to farm for profit under the conditions that now existed in Latium and Campania. For small estates he recommends the production of grapes, vegetables and olives rather than grain: a vineyard of 60 acres with 16 slaves, an olive grove of 160 acres with 13 slaves and contract labour at the height of the season, not to forget grazing on leased public land. His account shows the practical countryman, but—for all his praise of life on the land—not an old-fashioned landowner with his free peasants. He has in mind the city markets for wine and oil, vegetables and meat, leather and wool. This is the new farming which flourished on capital and slave labour by the mid century, and Cato was writing to advise his fellow senators about investment in agriculture. What then of the peasant farmers? Large numbers moved to the cities to find work. What of the military system, which rested upon property holders, not upon an urban proletariat? Here was the rub, as we have already seen. And the old relations of client loyalty? If these persisted after the peasants reached Rome,

they had become artificial, and it was a short step to paying for political support on the streets. We see slaves comprising the rural working class, even on the small estates. And in Etruria, southern Italy and Sicily, where great estates had long been in fashion, the influx of slaves allowed chain-gang methods with their accompaniment of brutality and savage resentment, which would issue in the slave wars of the latter part of the century. . . .

The situation in the middle of the second century B.C. is obscure; but it seems that economic progress continued in Rome, where the treasury still had ample reserves in 157; and we see the signs of Campanian prosperity in Pompeii. Italians went into trade in the east—as one can see at Delos—or moved north into the Po valley. The business class must have resented increasingly the pressure of senatorial control and they could appeal to popular support. The nobles applied their old methods: they prevented philosophers and rhetoricians from influencing the younger generation; in 154 the brilliant Diogenes, Critolaus and Carneades were not allowed to parade their learning when they visited Rome.

But towards 150 B.C. events took charge of Roman policy. The Spanish tribes had accepted a settlement at the hands of Sempronius Gracchus, but they would not tolerate misgovernment by the smaller men who succeeded him. In 154 B.C. the Lusitanians revolted and fought until 138, when they lost their leader Viriathus. In 153 the Celtiberians joined them and fought till 151, then again from 143 to 133, when Scipio Aemilianus finally crushed their resistance at Numantia. We need not follow the course of the Spanish wars, but we should ask some questions. Had there been injustice that called for remedy? In 149 the Lex Calpurnia would establish a court to handle cases of corrupt provincial administration. If Marcellus could negotiate a settlement in 151, why did the Senate not follow Gracchus' method of combining diplomacy with force? And how far had it calculated the cost in manpower of campaigns in central Spain? For although Roman military organization in the field was now professional, the levy of citizens for service was old-fashioned, and the reserve of qualified men was reduced. Overseas wars could not appeal to patriotism, as the wars against Carthage had done. Even if a citizen were liable for service during sixteen years, there must be a limit to any period of continuous campaigning. And if a man had served a period, how soon should he be recalled to the legions simply because he was an experienced soldier?

The Senate stood too firmly on the principle that it would accept no peace save a dictated one. The Roman people refused to be sacrificed to this policy in Spain. In the levy for 151 B.C. the tribunes of the plebs intervened to secure exemptions and ended by arresting the consuls, while the young nobles were reluctant to serve as officers. Lot was introduced to forestall discrimination at the expense of veterans, but Fabius in 145 and Pompeius in 140 had to be content with raw recruits. By this time the situation was out of hand, and in 138 tribunes would again intervene in a levy to arrest the consuls. However, it was the generals who disgraced the name of Rome. Lucullus and Galba treacherously violated the rules of war, Caepio and Pompeius arbitrarily repudiated treaties, and finally Mancinus made a humiliating surrender. A far cry from the resistance to Hannibal—but then we have tried to show that this was another age.

Meanwhile the Senate added to the black record. Conditions in Macedonia allowed the revolt of Andriscus, which was crushed in the Third Macedonian War (149–148 B.C.). Neglect in Greece encouraged the Achaean League to defy Rome, and in 146 Mummius destroyed Corinth. In North Africa trouble between Carthage and the expanding power of Numidia brought Roman intervention in the Third Punic War (149–146), and Scipio Aemilianus destroyed Carthage. The nobles, it is true, had differed about this policy, when Cato won the day, but the end of Carthage is marked by Roman bad faith. It is hard to find rational grounds for the death penalty on Corinth and Carthage, two great civilized cities. The Romans applied their old Samnite policy of annihilating opposition where it hindered their will—a brutal method, since they need not now seriously fear any threat to themselves. A policy with an irrational element in it? If this is so, it is because the Senate could hardly handle the combination of military problems that suddenly arose at this time. But these were problems that need not have become critical, had the nobles learnt the lessons of imperial responsibility. The Spanish tribes exacted the penalty. Above all, Rome would suffer at home, as Italian conditions degenerated and a slave war (135–132) broke out in Sicily, even before Tiberius Gracchus entered on his tribuneship.

The discontent in Rome about the military levies was only a symptom of the deep social unsettlement. The spread of large estates drove men off the land into the cities, where previously they had been attracted by the opportunities. The allied communities felt less secure in their relations with Rome, and arrogant Roman magistrates were less careful about respecting their local rights. In Rome the stringency of war conditions reduced the amenities of urban life, with its cheap corn and games, and the largess of wealthy patrons; the spoil from Corinth and Carthage afforded only temporary relief. And all the time unwilling citizens from the country were drafted into the army, while unhappy veterans returned to the cities with the violence and indiscipline of their soldiering. More seriously for Roman policy the nobles and the Senate had lost the authority of success. . . .

The leading Roman nobles had realized that the change in economic conditions in Italy was threatening the social basis of the military organization upon which they depended, and they still hoped to restore something like the old order. Yet the situation had become too complex for traditional thinking. Given time, could the Scipios and the Claudii have led Rome out of her impasse? Perhaps so in Italy, through painful negotiation with the allied authorities. Less likely in Rome, where the nobles were more firmly set against the equestrian class. But this is historical speculation: they were not given the time.

The traditions of the Roman ruling class were too strong, the social changes in Rome and Italy too deep; the very success of imperial expansion had intensified its own problems. Fifteen years would define the internal questions; it would be fifty years before Italy forced a decision upon Rome; and, as for the provinces, a century would elapse before the issues of power and responsibility were resolved.

Suggestions for Further Reading

Works that bear in some way or other on Rome's imperial expansion in the Republic are too numerous to catalogue exhaustively within a few pages. Some of the most important and influential studies, however, warrant mention. The Germans, as in all areas of classical scholarship, have been the most prolific producers. But English, French, Italian, and American scholars have contributed their share to an understanding of Roman overseas policy.

The chief sources of information on the period are the histories of Polybius and Livy. For the former, F. W. Walbank, *A Historical Commentary on Polybius* (vol. I, London, 1957; vol. II, London, 1967) is indispensable. The first two volumes have been published and take the story down to 196 B.C. This work is a careful, learned, and exhaustive commentary with full mastery of the literature on the subject. One might also consult Walbank's more general remarks in two articles: "Polybius and Rome's Eastern Policy," *Journal of Roman Studies,* LIII (1963), 1–13, and "Polybius,'" in *Latin Historians,* edited by T. A. Dorey (London, 1966), 39–63. A lengthy and recent analytical work on the historian is P. Pedech, *La méthode historique de Polybe* (Paris, 1964). Livy has been treated most lucidly and comprehensively by P. G. Walsh, *Livy, His Historical Aims and Methods* (London, 1961) and, in a shorter version, by Walsh, in the article "Livy," in *Latin Historians,* 115–142. On the sources utilized by Livy for his reconstruction, see A. Klotz, *Livius und seine Vorgänger* (Leipzig, 1940–1941).

For general works on Roman imperialism it will not be necessary to repeat titles from which selections are made in this book. W. Capelle, "Griechische Ethik und römischer Imperialismus," *Klio,* 25 (1932), 86–113, argues that

Rome derived her justification for empire from Greek ethical philosophy, concentrating on the theory that inferiors are best governed by their superiors. Others have stressed the elasticity of native Roman diplomatic categories and their adaptability to foreign relations, notably L. E. Matthaei, "On the Classification of Roman Allies," *Classical Quarterly,* 1 (1907), 182–204. The Germans have examined in detail and at length the legal forms adopted by Rome in dealing with overseas territories and developing diplomatic institutions. See especially E. Täubler, *Imperium Romanum* (Leipzig, 1913); A. Heuss, *Die völkerrechtlichen Grundlagen der römischen Aussenpolitik in republikanischer Zeit, Klio,* Beiheft 31 (Leipzig, 1931); and, most recently, W. Dahlheim, *Deditio und Societas: Untersuchungen zur Entwicklung der römischen Aussenpolitik in der Blütezeit der Republik* (Munich, 1965).

The Punic Wars have, of course, attracted much attention. The major general works are S. Gsell, *Histoire ancienne de l'Afrique du Nord,* 8 vols. (Paris, 1914-1928) and O. Meltzer, *Geschichte der Karthager,* 2 vols. (Berlin, 1879-1896). The third volume in the latter work, covering the period 218-146 B.C., is by U. Kahrstedt, (Berlin, 1913), who developed the theory that Rome's final destruction of Carthage was based on fear of a Numidian take-over in North Africa. A shorter but very useful and sensible account is B. H. Warmington, *Carthage* (New York, 1960).

A number of articles have focused on the controversial issues surrounding Rome's entrance into each of the three wars against Carthage. The reader's attention should be drawn to some of the most significant. M. Gelzer, "Römische Politik bei Fabius Pictor," *Hermes,* 68 (1933), 129–166, discusses the historiographical problems in ancient accounts of the First and Second Punic Wars. The question of whether or not Rome violated a treaty in initiating the First Punic War has long fostered scholarly debate. M. Cary, "A Forgotten Treaty between Rome and Carthage," *Journal of Roman Studies,* IX (1919), 67–77, argues vigorously that such a treaty was on the books. F. Schachermeyr, "Die römisch-punischen Verträge," *Rheinisches Museum für Philologie,* 79 (1930), 350–380, maintains that the so-called treaty was no more than a private agreement which had no binding effect. An important article by A. Heuss, "Der erste Punische Krieg und das Problem der römischen Imperialismus," *Historische Zeitschrift,* 169, (1949), 457–513, expresses doubts of the existence of a treaty. Heuss argues that Rome entered Sicily simply to protect Messana from the Greeks of Syracuse without anticipating conflict with Carthage. The war came as an accidental and unforeseen consequence.

The origins of the Hannibalic War, not dealt with in this book, have received extensive treatment elsewhere. As so often, controversy rages over the question of where to affix guilt. Did Hannibal stir up the war by crossing the Ebro River in Spain and encroaching on the Roman sphere of influence, or did Rome provoke hostilities by meddling in Saguntum, which was south of the Ebro? W. Hoffman, "Die römische Kriegserklärung an Karthago im Jahre 218," *Rheinisches Museum für Philologie,* 94 (1951), 69–88, argues for the Ebro crossing as the provocation for war. J. Carcopino, *Les Étapes de l'impérialisme romain,* 2d ed. (Paris, 1961), detects confusion in the sources over the location of the Ebro as a possible solution to the problem. Two recent articles, G. V. Sumner, "The Chronology of the Outbreak of the Second Punic War," *Proceedings of the African Classical Associations,* IX (1966), 5–30, and A. E. Astin, "Saguntum and the Origins of the Second Punic War," *Latomus,* XXVI (1967), 577–596, stress the significance of the Saguntum episode. An older contribution by W. Otto, "Eine antike Kriegsschuldfrage: Die Vorgeschichte des 2. Punischen Krieges," *Historische Zeitschrift,* 145 (1931), 489–516, eschews the ascription of guilt and the inevitability of the conflict, arguing

that neither side seemed anxious for the war until the final blowup.

Since the appearance of Kahrstedt's influential hypothesis on Rome's motives for the destruction of Carthage in 146, a large number of works have contributed to the debate. A few may be noted. C. Saumagne, "Les Pretextes juridiques de la IIIe guerre punique," *Revue Historique,* 167 (1931), 225–253, and 168 (1931), 1–42, offers a lengthy analysis of the legal aspects involved in Rome's relations with Carthage and Numidia, and stresses the ambiguous character of the Carthaginian "surrender" to Rome. W. Hoffman, "Die römische Politik des 2. Jahrhunderts und das Ende Karthagos," *Historia,* 9 (1960), 309–344, places Roman policy toward Carthage in the general context of her foreign policy, a harsher and more brutal attitude after 167 B.C. and a feeling that domination must be direct if it is to be successful. P. G. Walsh, "Massinissa," *Journal of Roman Studies,* 55 (1965), 149–160, takes very much this same line, adding that Massinissa goaded Rome into fear of Carthage, though the resultant destruction and annexation by Rome had not been his intention.

Contact and conflict between Rome and the Greek world has been among the most favored of classical subjects. The forceful and influential work of Maurice Holleaux, *Rome, la Grèce et les monarchies hellenistiques au IIIe siècle avant J.-C., 273–205* (Paris, 1921), is the obvious starting point. Holleaux carefully assesses all the evidence for Roman-Greek relations from the beginning, demonstrating the flimsy and dubious character of that evidence before the very end of the third century. The cause of Rome's first major venture into the east, the Macedonian war of 200–197, continues to be one of antiquity's most perplexing puzzles. Holleaux's case for preventive war has been restated and developed by A. H. McDonald and F. W. Walbank, "The Origins of the Second Macedonian War," *Journal of Roman Studies,* XXVII (1937), 180–207. A favorable but reserved critique of Holleaux may be found in J. Carcopino, *Les Étapes de l'impérialisme romain,* 2d ed. (Paris, 1961), in which the influence of Roman military men at work is seen in the policy of eastern

expansion. The detailed study by K. E. Pet-
zold, *Die Eröffnung des zweiten römisch-makedonisch-
en Krieges* (Berlin, 1940), argues that most of
the Roman justifications for war against Philip,
on the basis of obligations toward Greek allies
or friends, are *post eventum* fabrications by Roman apologists. On the other side, J. P. V. D.
Balsdon, "Rome and Macedon, 205–200 B.C.,"
Journal of Roman Studies, XLIV (1954), 30–42,
accepts the bulk of the tradition and empha-
sizes particularly Rome's willingness to heed
the appeals of Athens. A thorough reassessment
of the evidence and summary of all modern
opinion on the subject can be found in B. Ferro,
Le origini della seconda guerra macedonica (Palermo,
1960).

Roman relations with the Greek world became gradually more complex in the second
century B.C. Successes in the field may be attributed largely to the Roman military establishment, as discussed by A. Afzelius, *Die römische
Kriegsmacht während der Auseinandersetzung mit den
hellenistischen Grossmächten* (Copenhagen, 1944).
The steps toward conquest and hegemony are
carefully outlined by H. E. Stier, *Roms Aufsteig
zur Weltmacht und die griechische Welt* (Köln,
1957). For the rest, more specialized studies
have illuminated Roman dealings with particular states and areas in the Hellenic part of the
Mediterranean. Roman interests in Illyria and
in northwest Greece deserve emphasis as the
earliest stages of involvement with the Hellenistic powers. On this see especially S. I. Oost, *Roman Policy in Epirus and Acarnania in the Age of the
Roman Conquest of Greece* (Dallas, Tex., 1954) and
E. Badian, "Notes on Roman Policy in Illyria,
230–201 B.C., "*Papers of the British School at Rome,*"
XX (1952), 72–93. Macedon was a recurring
source of friction until its final subjugation in 146. F. W. Walbank, *Philip V of Macedon*
(Cambridge, 1940) is a comprehensive and invaluable treatment of that monarch's reign, the
critical period of Roman-Macedonian conflict.
And one should add also C. F. Edson, "Perseus
and Demetrius," *Harvard Studies in Classical
Philology,* XLVI (1935), 191–202, on growing
Roman intervention and the poisoning of relations with Macedon. The later period, to the
destruction of the Macedonian monarchy, is
treated by P. Meloni, *Perseo e la fine della monar-*

chia Macedone (Cagliari, Italy, 1953). On the
clash with Antiochus of Syria it will suffice to
acknowledge the excellent studies of A. Passer-
ini, "La pace con Filippo e le relazioni con Antioco," *Athenaeum,* 10 (1932), 105–126, and E
Badian, "Rome and Antiochus the Great," in
his *Studies in Greek and Roman History* (New York,
1964), 112–139. In Greece proper, with its divided and jealously bickering leagues and city-
states, Rome ran into countless difficulties. The
earliest stages are carefully analyzed by A. Ay-
mard, *Les Premiers Rapports de Rome et de la confédér-
ation achaienne* (Bordeaux, 1938). The development and techniques of Roman hegemony in
Greece receives treatment in J. A. O. Larsen,
"Was Greece Free Between 196 and 146?"
Classical Philology, XXX (1935), 193–214. Larsen's new book, *Greek Federal States* (Oxford,
1968) will unquestionably become the standard
work on that subject. Roman influence progressively expanded over other Hellenistic powers
in the Aegean and the eastern Mediterranean.
A number of particular studies elucidate the
development. For the kingdom of Pergamum,
see R. B. McShane, *The Foreign Policy of the Attalids of Pergamum* (Urbana, Ill., 1964); for the
cities of Asia Minor, see D. Magie, "Rome and
the City-States of Western Asia Minor from
200 to 133 B.C.," in *Anatolian Studies Presented to
W. H. Buckler* (Manchester, Eng., 1939),
161–185, and *Roman Rule in Asia Minor,* 2 vols.
(Princeton, N.J., 1950); for Rhodes, see H. H.
Schmitt, *Rom und Rhodos* (Munich, 1957); and
on relations with Egypt, see W. Otto, "Zur
Geschichte der Zeit des 6. Ptolemäers," *Abhand-
lungen der Bayerischen Akademie der Wissenschaften,
München,* 11 (1934), 1–147.

The researches of A. Schulten remain fundamental to a study of Roman policy in Spain.
Any number of his works can be cited. One
might note particularly *Numantia,* 3 vols. (Munich, 1905–1927), "Viriatus," *Neue Jahrbücher,*
39 (1917), 209–237, and *Geschichte von Numantia*
(Munich, 1933). The general summary provided by C. H. V. Sutherland, *The Romans in
Spain* (London, 1939), is also quite useful as an
introduction. A detailed study of the early pene-
tration by Rome in the Iberian Peninsula may
be found in K. Götzfried, *Annalen der römischen
Provinzen beider Spanien von der ersten Besetzung*

urch die Römer bis zum letzten grossen Freiheitskampf, 18–154 (Erlangen, Germany, 1907). For he later period one should consult the recent nd excellent book of H. Simon, *Roms Kriege in panien, 154–133 v. Chr.* (Frankfurt, 1962), which reats both the military and the political aspects f the struggle.

Finally, on the economic implications of Roaan imperialism, the careful, though skeptical, orks of Tenney Frank are essential reading. he collection of evidence in his *Economic Survey " Ancient Rome,* vol. I (Baltimore, Md., 1933), emains the standard reference work. The de-

velopment of his own arguments and conclusions may be found in his *Roman Imperialism* (New York, 1914) and *An Economic History of Rome to the End of the Republic* (Baltimore, Md., 1920). In addition, one can examine the material assembled by J. Hatzfeld, *Les Trafiquants italiens dans l'Orient hellénique* (Paris, 1919), and the analysis of H. Hill, *The Roman Middle Class in the Republican Period* (Oxford, 1952). On all these subjects, the interested student or scholar will find no dearth of stimulating reading matter.

735